Easy English

The Parts of Speech

Nancy Ragno

Cover Photo by Timur Kozmenko on Unsplash

CONTENTS

INTRODUCTION

The Vocabulary of English

Did you know that English has the largest and richest vocabulary of all European languages? The number of words in English is estimated to be more than a million, according to a four-year study by Harvard University and Google Books that analyzed the digital forms of over 5 million books (about 4% of all books ever published). The researchers tracked words and phrases that appeared in the books and how often they appeared. They found an estimated 1,022,000 unique words in English.

Of course, that does not mean that all of those words are still being used. Many are obsolete. About how many English words are currently in use? That is hard to say because English is a living language. New words are being added each year — many "borrowed" from other languages, while other words lose favor and are "retired."

How many words are listed in the dictionary? The 3rd (online) edition of the *Oxford English Dictionary* lists 171,476. entry words in current use. Of these, how many does the average English-speaking person know? The answer is about 20,000 for the average speaker and about 40,000 for university-educated speakers. But for ordinary speaking and writing, most people use about 5,000 very common words and use them repeatedly.

The Parts of Speech

The vast array of word choices is a great boon for writers; but it may seem daunting to anyone learning English. The good news for English learners is that all the words in English can be separated into eight categories. These eight categories are known as the *parts of speech*, and they are based on the eight kinds of "jobs" words perform in sentences.

Eight Parts of Speech

The parts of speech are:
1. nouns
2. verbs
3. pronouns
4. adjectives
5. adverbs
6. prepositions
7. conjunctions
8. interjections.

These parts of speech are the building blocks of grammar, the building blocks of sentences. The most important parts of speech are nouns and verbs. In fact, the verb is the only part of speech that must be in a sentence. It is essential to the sentence's meaning.

One thing to keep in mind is that the meaning of a word does not necessarily determine its part of speech. A word's part of speech is determined by its use in a sentence. Some words can be used as different parts of speech and have different meanings. The word "fast," for example, can be used as a noun, verb, adjective, or adverb.

Why Learn the Parts of Speech?

Learning the parts of speech and how they are used will help you to:
1. Understand the structure of a language – its grammar, how the language is put together
2. Achieve clarity in your speech and writing

3. Spot mistakes in grammar and understand
why they are incorrect

4. Understand grammar instruction

5. Study, discuss, and ask questions about
English because you know and understand
the terminology

6. Increase your self-confidence in speaking and
writing

7. Avoid embarrassing errors in English

If English Is Not Your Native Language

Learning the parts of speech is especially valuable if English is not your native language. It will increase your speed in learning English and increase your reading and listening comprehension.

As you learn English, pay close attention to ways in which the *grammar* (structure) of your native language and English are different. It is these differences that may very well cause errors in learning to use "correct" English.

Word Order in English. English is one of the languages that uses *word order* to show the functions of the words in its sentences. English has what is called *natural word order*. In general, this is: *subject – verb – object*. (See the chapter on verbs for more on this.) Many languages, however, do not use word order as a basis for grammar. Instead, they have a flexible word order and *add endings* to words to show their function and meaning in a sentence. Such languages are called *inflected languages*. Students studying an inflected language have many word endings to learn and memorize. In contrast, students of English have only a few endings to learn:

for example, the *s* for a noun plural and *d* for the past tense of a verb.

What are some examples of inflected languages? In Europe, they include French, Spanish, Portuguese, Greek, German, Italian, Polish, Finnish, Czech, Hungarian, Lithuanian, Romanian, and Russian. The main language of India, Hindi, is also an inflected language.

Imagine being a student of Hungarian. You would need to learn up to 238 possible forms for nouns. Spanish has up to 50 forms for verbs. Fortunately for the ESL student, English is a weakly inflected language with few word endings. Word order, on the other hand, is important in English.

Grammatical Gender. Some languages have grammar systems that assign gender to its nouns (name words). This is true even for inanimate objects, which have no gender. In Italian, for example, the word for "garden" is a masculine noun; the word for "fountain" is a feminine noun. The form of words associated with the noun (e.g., "the") must match the gender of the noun.

About half the languages in the world use this grammatical gender. English is not one of them. Instead, English uses "natural gender." Inanimate objects are not referred to as "he" or "she," but as "it." Keep this in mind if your native language uses grammatical gender.

Throughout the book you will find additional suggestions for ESL students.

The parts of speech are the building blocks of sentences. They are important in learning a new language. Becoming familiar with the parts of speech will speed up your understanding of English and your ability to use it.

This book is designed to explain the parts of speech quickly and clearly. Traditionally, the parts of speech have been taught by applying terms from the grammar of Latin – *subjunctive, indicative, gerund, infinitive, present participle, reflexives, intransitive, future perfect progressive* – to name a few. This practice started with 18th century grammarians. But English is a Germanic language, not Latin. It is a stretch to apply Latin terms to English grammar. First of all, they are not immediately understandable to speakers of English. They need to be explained. Chances are, they are seldom used outside of English class and are soon forgotten.

Nevertheless, in order to study and talk about English, it is necessary to become acquainted with grammar terminology, just as it is necessary to know math terminology to understand mathematics and the table of periodic elements to study chemistry.

Grammar is such a broad topic that it can't all be covered and explained clearly in a book of this type. This book is not a complete grammar textbook. It is not a complete grammar reference. Instead, this book is an easy-to-use reference guide on grammar basics: *the parts of speech.* In this book you'll learn to identify the parts of speech and know how and when to use each kind. *Easy English: The Parts of Speech* is designed to quickly explain grammar terminology, rules, and guidelines and to give you practice in using them.

How the book is organized. This book is organized in chapters that *you don't have to do in order.* There are eight chapters, one for each part of speech. Each chapter ends with a chapter quiz and end-of-chapter exercises. Quizzes are designed to make it fast and easy to check your understanding of the part of speech discussed in the chapter. You may decide to take the chapter quiz before reading the chapter. This will show what you already know about that part of speech and what you need to focus on. (Or, you may discover that you do not need to study that chapter!) Answers are provided after each quiz.

Suggestions for Using the Book

1. You may decide to read through the book first and then use it as a handy reference guide to the parts of speech.

2. You do not need to read the chapters in order. Skip around as much as you like.

3. Use the book as a quick review of grammar terminology and the parts of speech.

4. You may decide to start by taking the end-of-chapter quiz before reading the chapter. This will enable you to find out what you already know and what you are unclear about and need to review or focus on.

Once the grammar has been learned, writing is simply talking on paper and in time learning what not to say.
-- Beryl Bainbridge

Grammar is to a writer what anatomy is to a sculptor or the scales to a musician. You may loathe it, it may bore you, but nothing will replace it, and once mastered it will support you like a rock.
— B. J. Chute

NOUNS

A noun is a word that names a person, place, thing, or idea.

In order to communicate, or even think, we need names for the things in this world — not only in the physical world, but in the world of ideas, theories, concepts. Every language has developed names. In English, name words are called *nouns.*

Appropriately, the word *noun* comes from the Latin word *nomen,* meaning "name."

Nouns are basic to language. It is not surprising that they make up over 70% of the vocabulary of English. Nouns are one of the two basic building blocks of the English sentence. (The other is verbs.)

KINDS OF NOUNS

To simplify the study of English grammar, nouns are divided into these groups:

1. concrete and abstract nouns

2. common and proper nouns

3. compound nouns

4. collective nouns

5. count and noncount nouns.

Why is it helpful to learn about these classifications? Learning about them helps you avoid mistakes in the capitalization of nouns and in the agreement of nouns and verbs in your sentences.

CONCRETE AND ABSTRACT NOUNS

Nouns name things that exist in the physical world, things we can observe with our senses. These are called *concrete nouns*. Nouns also name things that exist in the world of thought, things (such as thoughts) that are real but cannot be perceived by the senses. These nouns are called *abstract nouns*.

Concrete Nouns

Concrete nouns name people, places, and things that can be perceived by any of the of the senses — sight, hearing, smell, taste, or touch. (Think of *concrete:* the stone-like building material. It can be seen, touched. smelled and even tasted.) See examples in the following table.

18

Concrete Nouns		
Persons	**Places**	**Things**
physician	city	whale
child	lake	nose
musician	country	arrow
explorer	suburbs	computer
lawyer	beach	voice
neighbor	restaurant	medicine
teenager	zoo	perfume

Abstract Nouns

Abstract nouns name things that are not physical. Although they are not perceived by the senses, they exist in the mind. See the table below.

Abstract Nouns		
wish	hope	theory
love	joy	fear
democracy	arithmetic	harmony
courage	ambition	pity
virtue	hate	devotion
eternity	jealousy	freedom

COMMON AND PROPER NOUNS

Nouns are also classified as *common nouns* and *proper nouns.* Look at the table below. See if you can deduce the difference between common nouns and proper nouns and how they are written.

	COMMON NOUN	PROPER NOUN
Persons	woman	Emily Dickinson
Places	country	Brazil
Things	book	The Hobbit
Ideas	month	November

Common Nouns

In general, *common nouns* are commonly used, general names. They do not specify one specific person, place, thing, or idea. Common nouns are not capitalized.

Examples:

> dentist, wood, bird, speech, door, dancer, ant, democracy, wish, nail, hamburger

Proper Nouns

Proper nouns are names of *specific* persons, places, things, or ideas. Proper nouns are capitalized.
Examples:

> Mark Twain, Alabama, Jeffrey, New Orleans, Mount Rushmore, Halloween, United States

COMPOUND NOUNS

A compound noun is a noun formed by joining two or more nouns. Some compound nouns keep the nouns separated (e.g., *hot dog*). These are *open compounds*. Other compounds are written as one word (e.g., *toothache*). These are *closed compounds*.

Still other compounds are hyphenated. These are called *hyphenated compounds*.

COMPOUND NOUNS		
OPEN COMPOUNDS	full moon attorney general ginger ale	hot dog student nurse egg rolls
CLOSED COMPOUNDS	bedroom toothache grandfather	keyboard checkbook sunrise
HYPHENATED COMPOUNDS	mother-in-law three-year-old check-up	middle-school one-half vice-president

How can you tell if a compound noun should be open, closed, or hyphenated? There are no rules . If you are unsure, check with a dictionary.

COLLECTIVE NOUNS

Think of a collective noun as the name for a collection, or group, of people or things. For example, the word *team* is a collective noun that represents a group of players on the same side in a game. The word *class* is a collective noun that represents a group of students. Collective nouns for general groups of people include: *audience, company, society, crowd, group, people, gang.*

In addition, English has nouns for unique groups of people, groups in which all members share one thing in common. For example, a group of sailors is called a *crew*; a group of actors is called a *troupe*.

Do you want to expand your vocabulary? Some unusual collective nouns are listed below.

COLLECTIVE NOUNS	
A group of _____	**is called a _____.**
witches	coven
philosophers	confusion
teachers	quiz
writers	worship
vegetarians	sprig
painters	curse
experts	discord
golfers	lie
pianists	pound
bakers	tabernacle
barbers	babble
cooks	hastiness
professors	pomposity
joggers	wheeze

Collective nouns for general groups of *things* include: *bunch, pair, collection,* and *set.* Other collective nouns are more specific. See the table on the next page for examples. (Collective nouns are in italics.)

COLLECTIVE NOUNS FOR THINGS	
a *bar*	of soap
a *quiver*	of arrows
a *bushel*	of apples
a *belt*	of asteroids
a *hill*	of beans
a *fright*	of ghosts
a *bank*	of circuits
a *mess*	of grits
a *morning*	of hammers
a *clutch*	of eggs
a *lot*	of salt
a *crash*	of software
a *patter*	of footsteps
a *hassle*	of errands
a *maze*	of canyons
an *accompaniment*	of condiments

Collective nouns for *animals* are not only numerous, but often surprising and downright funny. Here are a few examples.

a *gaggle* of geese

a *shrewdness* of apes

an *unkindness* of ravens

a *clowder* of cats

a *kindle* of kittens

a *quiver* of cobras

an *exaltation* of larks

a *bask* of crocodiles

a *shiver* of sharks

a *quiver* of cockroaches

a *business* of flies

a *bloom* of jellyfish

a consortium of crabs

a *hood* of snails
a *tower* of giraffes

NOTE: Even though a collective noun stands for more than one person, place or thing, a collective noun is usually *singular* and takes a *singular verb.*

COUNT AND NONCOUNT NOUNS

A **count noun**, as you probably suspect, is a noun that names something that can be counted. The noun *car*, for example, is a count noun. You can count *one* car, *two* cars, *three* cars, and so on.

A count noun is preceded by **a, an**, or **the**. (*An* is used instead of *a* if the next word begins with a vowel sound.)

Examples:

>*a* book, *an* egg
>*the* book, *the egg*

A count noun usually has both a singular and a plural form.

Examples:

>*a* tree (singular); *the* trees (plural)
>*an* apple (singular); *the* apples (plural)

Just as a count noun names something that can be counted, a **noncount noun** names something that can't be counted. The word *milk,* for example is a noncount noun. You can't count milk: *one* milk, *two* milks, *three* milks, and so on.

A noncount noun may be preceded by *the*, but NOT by *a* or *an*.

>*Correct*: *the* rice; *the* air
>*Incorrect*: *a* rice; *an* air

A noncount noun is *always* singular and takes a singular verb.

>*Correct*: The oxygen *is . . .*
>*Incorrect*: The oxygen *are . . .*

The Articles *a, an,* and *the*

Why can't a noncount noun be preceded by *a* or *an*? Because *a* and *an* stand for the number *one. A* book is *one* book. *An* apple is *one* apple. Since *a* and *an* stand for the number *one*, and noncount nouns can't be counted with numbers, a noncount noun can't be preceded by *a* or *an*.

Why does it matter if a noun is a count noun or a noncount noun? It matters in order to choose the correct *article* that comes before it. The articles are the words *a, an,* and *the.* They are also called "noun markers" because they mark, or show, that a noun follows.

Whether a noun is a count noun or noncount noun also matters when deciding whether the noun takes a singular or plural verb. (See the chapter on verbs for more about this.)

NOTE: If English is not your native language,283 be aware that count and noncount nouns are not the same in all languages. Japanese, for example, does not have count nouns. Some words that are noncount words in English may be count words in other languages. (Examples include: *hair, information, homework.*)

MAKING NOUNS PLURAL

Most nouns have forms for the singular and plural. A *singular* noun represents *one* person, place, idea, or thing; a *plural* noun represents *more than one.*

REGULAR PLURALS

Add *-s* or *-es*

In general, add *-s* or *-es* to a singular noun to make it plural: *dog* (one dog); *dog**s*** (more than one dog); *fox* (one fox); *fox**es*** (more than one fox).

Nouns Ending in *s, z, x, ch,* or *sh*

If a noun ends in *s, z, x, ch, or sh,* add *-es* to form the plural. The reason for this spelling rule becomes evident if you add an -*s* to a word ending in *s, z, x, ch, or sh* and then try to pronounce it. It is impossible.

The table below gives some examples of adding -*es* to form the plural of nouns

.

Singular	Plural
arch	arches
beach	beaches
box	boxes
branch	branches
church	churches
dish	dishes
dress	dresses
fox	foxes
glass	glasses
guess	guesses
Mr. Jones	the Joneses
speech	speeches
tax	taxes
waltz	waltzes

Nouns Ending in *-f or -fe*

If a noun ends in *-f* or *-fe*, change *-f* or *-fe* to -*ves* to form the plural. Again, the reason for this spelling rule is for the sake of making the plural noun easy to pronounce. See the following table for examples.

Singular	Plural
wolf	wolves
shelf	shelves
knife	knives
life	lives
leaf	leaves
wife	wives
half	halves
calf	calves
hoof	hooves
loaf	loaves

A few nouns ending in *-f* form the plural by adding *-s*: brief/brief**s**; chief/chief**s**; gulf/gulf**s**.

Nouns Ending in *o*

If a noun ends in *-o* preceded by a consonant, add **-es** to form the plural.

Singular	Plural
echo	echoes
hero	heroes
potato	potatoes
tomato	tomatoes
volcano	volcanoes
mosquito	mosquitoes
domino	dominoes
embargo	embargoes

Nouns Ending in *y*

If a noun ends in *y* preceded by a *consonant*, change the *y* to *i* and add *-es* to form the plural. See the two tables that follow for examples.

Singular	Plural
berry	berries
story	stories
puppy	puppies
city	cities
enemy	enemies
sky	skies
penny	pennies
library	libraries
hobby	hobbies
family	families
duty	duties

Singular	Plural
ray	rays
boy	boys
donkey	donkeys
attorney	attorneys
chimney	chimneys
turkey	turkeys
valley	valleys
birthday	birthdays
toy	toys
key	keys
essay	essays

PLURALS ENDING IN *-EN*

The use of the regular plural endings *-s* and *-es* did not come into widespread use in England until the 14th century. In the 13th century **-en** was a common plural ending – especially in Southern England. Today, some eight hundred years later, only a few of those *-en* plural words still survive. They are: *ox/oxen; brother/ brethren; child/children.*

IRREGULAR PLURALS

A number of nouns do not form the plural by adding the regular plural ending *-s* or *-es*. They are irregular plural nouns, meaning that they do not form their plurals in the regular, or usual, way.

30

SUGGESTION: There are many irregular plural nouns. Unfortunately, there are no infallible rules for them. To prevent spelling errors, memorize the spellings of irregular plurals you use. If you are unsure of a plural's spelling, look it up. When you are writing on a computer, a spell-check program will alert you to possible spelling errors.

Plurals Formed by Vowel Changes

Some words form their plurals by changing the vowel sound in the middle of the word. Why? Because English has German roots, and German changes the middle vowel sound of a noun to make it plural. In today's English, we still retain some of these irregular plurals. See the table below for examples.

Singular	Plural
man	men
woman	women
foot	feet
tooth	teeth
louse	lice
mouse	mice
goose	geese

Nouns with Foreign Plurals

English has "borrowed" words from many languages. Some English nouns of foreign origin have retained the foreign spelling of their plurals. Others have been Anglicized and form plurals by adding -*s* or -*es*. Still others have two plurals — an Anglicized plural as well as the original foreign plural. When in doubt about which plural is preferred, check a dictionary. Most dictionaries list the preferred spelling first.

See the table below for some general guidelines on how to form foreign plurals:

NOUNS WITH SPECIAL PLURAL FORMS	
a **to** ae	If the noun ends in *a*, change *a* to *ae*: *alumna/alumnae*.
us **to** i	If the noun ends in *us*, change *us* to *i*: *alumnus/alumni*
is **to** es	If the noun ends in *is*, *change is* to *es*: *crisis/crises*.
on **to** a	If the noun ends in *on*, change *on* to *a*: *phenomenon/phenomena*.
um **to** a	If the noun ends in *um*, *change um* to *a*: *bacterium/bacteria*.
ix/ex **to** ices/exes	If the noun ends in *ix* or *ex*, change *ix* or *ex* to *ices* or *exes*: *index/indices*
o **to** i	If the noun ends in *o*, change the *o* to *i*: *libretto/libretti*; *graffito/graffiti*
eau **to** eaux	If the noun ends in *eau*, change the *eau* to *eaux*: *plateau/plateaux*

Nouns with the Same Singular & Plural

Some nouns have the same form for both the singular and plural. See the following table for some common examples.

The Same in Singular and Plural			
deer	sheep	swine	salmon
trout	grass	vermin	fish
grapefruit	aircraft	scissors	shrimp
offspring	scissors	species	glasses

Noncount Nouns

REMINDER: Noncount nouns are always singular. They have no plural.

Compound Nouns

Plurals of compound nouns can be tricky. Which word in the compound is made plural? Some guidelines are given below

Closed Compounds (written as one word). Make the final word of the compound plural, usually by adding -s or -es.
Examples:
armful/armfuls, eyelash/eyelashes, flashback/flashbacks, foothold/footholds, grandchild/grandchildren, mousetrap/mousetraps, teaspoonful/teaspoonfuls, toothbrush/toothbrushes, wineglass/wineglasses

Open and Hyphenated Compounds (written as separate or hyphenated words): An open or hyphenated compound is formed by a noun and one or more modifiers. Make the noun plural. The noun is the chief element in the compound.

<u>*Examples*</u>:
    editor-in-chief/ editors-in-chief
    assistant attorney/assistant attorneys
    daughter-in-law/daughters-in-law,
    major general/major generals
    runner-up/runners/up

PLURALS OF PROPER NOUNS

The plurals of all proper nouns are formed by the addition of *-s* to the singular, unless the *-s* sound adds another syllable. In that case the plural is formed by adding *-es*. (Don't use an apostrophe to make a name plural.)

Here are some examples of proper noun plurals:

the Woodfords	*the McFarlands*	*the IBMs*
the Intels	*the Giamos*	*the Reeves*
the Mugfords	*the Ricardos*	*the Nickells*

MAKING NOUNS POSSESSIVE

A noun can show ownership by *adding an apostrophe-s* or an *apostrophe* to the end of the noun.

For example, in "*Karen's coat*," the *apostrophe-s* shows that the coat belongs to Karen.

In "*children's game*," the *apostrophe-s* shows that the games are for the children.

In "James' homework," the apostrophe shows that the homework belongs to James.

Singular Noun	Possessive Noun
boy	boy's
fox	fox's
deer	deer's
thief	thief's
man	man's
Wilson	Wilson's

POSSESSIVES OF SINGULAR NOUNS

The simple rule on how to make a singular noun possessive is: *Add apostrophe-s to the noun.*
If the noun already ends in *s*, you may either *add apostrophe-s* or simply *add an apostrophe.*

Singular Noun	Possessive Noun
princess	princess's *or* princess'
class	class's *or* class'
Rogers	Rogers's *or* Rogers'
Cortez	Cortez's *or* Cortez'
Stradivarius	Stradivarius's *or* Stradivarius'

POSSESSIVES OF PLURAL NOUNS

If the plural form of a noun does *not* end in *s*, *add -apostrophe-s* to form the possessive.

Plural Noun	Plural Possessive
men	men's
children	children's
women	women's
oxen	oxen's
geese	geese's
alumni	alumni's

If the plural form of a noun already ends in *s, add an apostrophe only.* (Strictly speaking, *adding apostrophe-s* to a noun ending in *s* is not incorrect. It is, however, difficult to pronounce, so it is preferable to simply add an apostrophe.)

Plural Noun	Plural Possessive
boys	boys'
foxes	foxes'
thieves	thieves'
turkeys	turkeys'
Wilsons	Wilsons'
Joneses	Joneses'

POSSESSIVES OF COMPOUND NOUNS

To make a compound noun possessive, *add apostrophe-s to the last word.* This is true for both singular and plural possessives, as well as for the names of organizations and companies.

Compound Noun	Possessive Form
mother-in-law	mother-in-law's
mothers-in-law	mothers-in-law's
someone else	someone else's
Rise-and-Shine Club	Rise-and-Shine Club's
hamburger	hamburger's
General Electric	General Electric's

What about joint ownership? That is, what if two or more people (or things) own something? In that case, only make the last noun possessive: e.g., *"Pat and George's boat."*

Never use abstract nouns when concrete ones will do. If you mean "More people died," don't say "Mortality rose.
— C. S. Lewis

CHAPTER 1

NOUNS: CHECK-UP

(Scroll down for answers.)

Concrete and Abstract Nouns

Write the nouns in each paragraph. After each noun, write whether it is a concrete noun or an abstract noun.

1. Botanists say that tomatoes are not vegetables, as many people think. Instead, they are fruits because they contain seeds.
2. The ears of a grasshopper are on the sides of its abdomen.
3. The confusion and chaos caused by their arrival only increased my nervousness and anxiety.
4. Scientists in France made a groundbreaking discovery. Fleas can jump farther and higher on a dog than on a cat.
5. In a ritual held at the beginning of spring, Japanese toss soybeans around their houses for luck. The participants then pick up and eat a bean for each year of their lives.

Common and Proper Nouns

1. Determine the proper nouns you found in exercises 1-5 above.
2. Write a proper noun for each of these common nouns. (Invent a name if you wish.): (a) woman; (b) man, (c) street, (d) school, (e) holiday, (f) book.

Compound Nouns
Complete the following paragraph with the correct
compound nouns listed below it. If you are unsure of
the noun's correct form, check in a dictionary.

(1)! Tim, my **(2)**, a **(3)**, dropped my **(4)** in a
(5). Fortunately, a **(6)** retrieved it. But did I
have an **(7)**? I had to reach my **(8)**. Would I
need new **(9)**? Must I install new **(10)**? So many
problems! Such a **(11)**!

1. Teen-agers; Teen agers; Teenagers
2. grandson; grand son; grandson
3. fifteen year old; fifteenyearold; fifteen-year-old
4. (a) cell-phone; (b) cell phone; (c) cell phone
5. (a) swimming pool; (b) swimmingpool; (c)
   swimming-pool
6. (a) life guard; (b) lifeguard; (c) life-guard
7. (a) Internet-connection; (b) Internetconnection;
   (c)Internet connection
8. (a) website; (b) web site; (c) web-site
9. (a) passwords; (b) pass words; (c) pass-words
10. (a) soft ware; (b) soft-ware; (c) software
11. (a) head-ache; (b) headache; (c) head ache

Collective Nouns
Identify the collective nouns in the following
sentences:

1. Our family is not very large.
2. The club meets once a month.
3. Are you a member of the committee?
4. The class lasts two hours.
5. A herd of deer grazed near the brook.

Count and Noncount Nouns

Identify the count and noncount nouns in the following sentences.

1. How much water is in a glass of milk?
2. How do fish get oxygen?
3. Tests showed excessive pollution in our air and lakes.
4. First remove the grime on the house before you apply paint.
5. This car runs on both gas and electricity.

Making Nouns Plural

Write the plural of each of the following nouns:

house, asteroid, branch, cafeteria, lullaby, thief, potato, shrimp, tooth, man, crisis, alumna, index, grandchild, butterfly, speech, leaf, knife, echo, shampoo, man-of-war

Making Nouns Possessive

Write the singular and plural possessives of each of the following nouns:

woman, salmon, kitten, mouse, baby, mother-in-law, donkey, trout, sheep, scientist, wife, rodeo, theory, girl, bird

CHAPTER 1

NOUNS: ANSWERS

Concrete and Abstract Nouns

1. Botanists (concrete), tomatoes (concrete), vegetables (concrete), fruits (concrete), seeds (concrete)
2. ears (concrete), grasshopper (concrete), sides (concrete), abdomen (concrete)
3. confusion (abstract), chaos (abstract), arrival (abstract), nervousness (abstract), anxiety (abstract)
4. Scientists (concrete), France (concrete), discovery (abstract), fleas (concrete), dog (concrete), cat (concrete)
5. ritual (abstract), beginning (abstract), spring (abstract), Japanese (concrete), soybeans (concrete), houses (concrete), luck(abstract), participants (concrete), bean (concrete), year (abstract), lives (abstract)

Common and Proper Nouns

1. France, Japanese
2. Answers will vary, but each should be capitalized.

Compound Nouns

Teenagers! Tim, my grandson, a fifteen-year-old, dropped my cellphone in a swimming pool. Fortunately. a lifeguard retrieved it. But did I have an Internet connection? I had to reach my website. Would I need new passwords? Must I install new software? So many problems! Such a headache!

Collective Nouns

1. family
2. club
3. committee
4. class
5. herd

Count and Noncount Nouns

1. water (noncount); glass (count); milk (noncount)
2. fish (count); oxygen (noncount)
3. tests (count); pollution (noncount); air
   (noncount); lakes (count)
4. grime (noncount); house (count); paint
   (noncount)
5. car (count); gas (noncount); electricity (noncount)

Making Nouns Plural

houses, asteroids, branches, cafeterias, lullabies,
thieves, potatoes, shrimp, teeth, men, crises,
alumnae, indexes or indices (either is correct),
grandchildren, butterflies, speeches, leaves, knives,
echoes, shampoos, men-of-war

Making Nouns Possessive

woman's/women's; salmon's/salmon's;
kitten's/kittens'; mouse's/mice's; baby's/babies';
mother-in-law's/mothers-in-law's;
donkey's/donkeys'; trout's/trout's; sheep's/sheep's;
scientist's/scientists'; wife's/wives'; rodeo's/rodeos';
theory's/theories'; girl's/girls'; bird's/birds'

PRONOUNS

A pronoun is a word that is used in place of a noun or nouns.

The word *pronoun* comes from the Latin words *pro,* meaning "for," and *nomen,* meaning "name." Thus, a pronoun is a word used *for* (in place of) a *noun* (name).

Examples of Pronouns:

> I, you, he, she, it, we, they, him, her, them, my, mine, his, her, its, your, their, us, ours

WHY ARE PRONOUNS NEEDED?

Consider the paragraphs below. The first paragraph is an excerpt based on Lewis Carroll's *Alice's Adventures in Wonderland.* But the pronouns have been removed and replaced with the nouns they stand for. The second paragraph is as Carroll wrote it. The pronouns are in bold type.

Without pronouns:
Alice was beginning to get very tired of sitting by Alice's sister on the bank, and of having nothing to do. Once or twice Alice had peeped into the book Alice's sister was reading, but the book had no pictures or conversation in the book.

With pronouns:
Alice was beginning to get very tired of sitting by **her** sister on the bank; and of having nothing to do. Once or twice **she** had peeped into the book

her sister was reading, but **it** had no pictures or conversation in **it**.

Notice how pronouns are used to avoid needless, tiresome repetition of the same nouns. Imagine how stilted and awkward our speech and writing would be without the use of pronouns.

WHY STUDY PRONOUNS?

The main reason to study pronouns is to avoid errors in grammar. One of the most common errors in English grammar is *using the wrong pronoun.* Pronouns have different forms (e.g., singular and plural; subject and object). The forms of pronouns must match, or *agree* with, the nouns they replace. If the wrong pronoun is used, the reader or listener will not know what the pronoun stands for and will be confused.

WORD ORDER: PRONOUNS AND ANTECEDENTS

Antecedent Comes First

Where do you put a pronoun in a sentence? In most cases, the pronoun's *antecedent* must be named first. A pronoun's antecedent is the noun (person, place, or thing) the pronoun stands for. That noun must be mentioned earlier in the sentence or paragraph before it can be replaced with a pronoun. Otherwise, how would anyone know what word the pronoun replaces?

After the antecedent has been named, the pronoun can be used to replace it. The antecedent may be in the same sentence or a few sentences before its pronoun, as long as it's clear which noun the pronoun replaces.

Have you ever been reading conversation in a novel and suddenly realize you don't know who is speaking or what "it" refers to? This happens because, for example, the writer has used "she said" without making it clear who "she" stands for; or the writer has mentioned "it" without making it clear what "it" is. The result? The reader is confused. This kind of writer's error is called "faulty pronoun reference."

In the illustration above, *Kelly* is the antecedent of the pronouns *she* and *her*.

WORD HISTORY

Antecedent: The word *antecedent* comes from the Latin words *ante*, meaning "before" and *cedere*, meaning "go." An antecedent "goes before" the pronoun that replaces it.

Pronouns Without Antecedents

Some pronouns do not need antecedents because their meaning is clear. The pronoun *I*, for example, almost never has an antecedent because it is clear that *I* refers to the writer/speaker. Likewise, the pronoun *you* seldom has an antecedent.

KINDS OF PRONOUNS

There are six types, or classes, of pronouns:
1. Personal Pronouns
2. Reflexive and Intensive Pronouns
3. Relative Pronouns
4. Demonstrative Pronouns
5. Interrogative Pronouns
6. Indefinite Pronouns.

PERSONAL PRONOUNS

Personal Pronouns are the common, everyday pronouns we use to stand for persons and things. What does the term *personal pronoun* mean? The word *personal* is a little misleading here because it doesn't have the common meaning of "private" or "of a particular person." *Person* has a special meaning in grammar and in writing. It refers to either: (1) the *person* speaking [the *First Person*]; (2) the *person or persons* spoken to [the *Second Person*]; or (3) the *persons* or *things* spoken about [the *Third Person*].

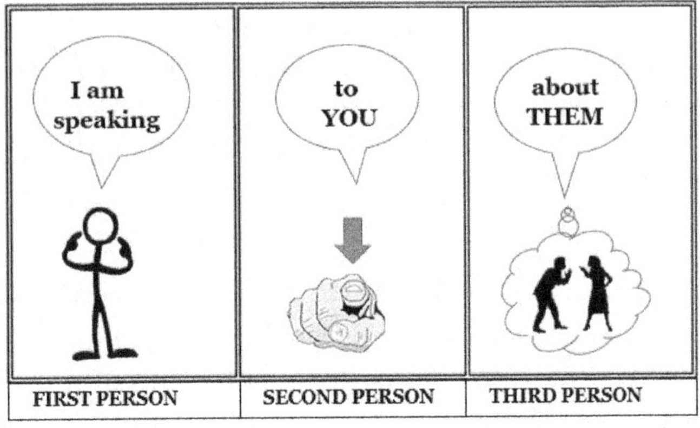

The personal pronouns are listed in the table below. Notice that there are singular, plural, and possessive forms.

	SINGULAR	PLURAL
FIRST PERSON (person speaking)	I, me	we, us
Possessives:	my, mine	our, ours
SECOND PERSON (person spoken to)	you	you
Possessives:	your, yours	your, yours
THIRD PERSON (person or thing spoken about)	she, her he, him it	they, them
Possessives:	her, hers his its	their, theirs

First-Person Pronouns

Writing in the first person. Writers use first-person pronouns to write about themselves, their thoughts, their emotions. In an autobiography, for example, the author tells the story of his or her own life, using the pronouns *I, me, my,* and *mine* to stand for his or her name. "I" indicates that it is the author who is speaking. This writing style is called writing in the *first person.* Authors also write in the first person to tell a story from the point of view of one character in a story. In the novel *Moby Dick,* for example, Herman Melville has the character Ishmael introduce himself and then tell his story. In this excerpt, notice how Melville uses first-person pronouns to show that Ishmael is telling the story.

> Call **me** Ishmael. Some years ago — never mind how long precisely — having little or no money in **my** purse, and nothing particular to interest **me** on shore, **I** thought **I** would sail about a little and see the watery part of the world.
> — *Moby Dick* by Herman Melville

Second-Person Pronouns

Writing in the second person. The second-person pronoun is ***you***. Its possessive forms are ***your*** and ***yours***. These forms are the same in both singular and plural. The second person is used to speak directly to someone else. "***I*** (*the speaker*) am speaking to ***you*** (*the listener or listeners*)."

Writers use the second-person, *you*, to address readers directly. This technique is termed "writing in the *second person.*" Books of instruction and self-help books are often written in the second person. Occasionally fiction is written in the second person. Here is an example from the children's book *Oh, the Places You'll Go!* by Dr. Seuss. Notice how Dr. Seuss uses the pronouns *you* and *your* to speak directly to you, the reader.

> **You** have brains in **your** head. **You** have feet in **your** shoes. **You** can steer **your**self any direction **you** choose. **You**'re on **your** own. And **you** know what **you** know. And **YOU** are the guy who'll decide where to go.
> *Oh, the Places You'll Go!* by Dr. Seuss

Third-Person Pronouns

Third-person pronouns stand for the names of persons or things *spoken about*. The third-person pronouns are listed in the table below. Notice that there are forms for singular and plural, possessive, and gender (masculine, feminine, neutral).

Third-Person Pronouns	
Singular	**Plural**
he, him (*masculine*) she. her (feminine) it (*neutral*)	they, them
Possessives	
his (*masculine*) her, hers (*feminine*) its (*neutral*)	their, theirs

They" as a Singular Pronoun, Neutral Gender

Before 2019, the following sentence would be considered incorrect: "Each taxpayer needs to file **their** tax return by April 15." Grammarians would say that since *taxpayer* is singular, its pronoun must be singular. The sentence should be: "Each taxpayer must file **his or her** tax return by April 15." The trouble is, people don't talk that way. From medieval manuscripts we know that people have been using *they* as a singular neutral pronoun since the 13th century. Later, the pronoun *he* was used as a singular neutral pronoun. But using *he* for everyone seemed to exclude women. Thus, *he or she* became the rule in formal writing.

Writers find the *he or she* construction awkward and cumbersome. It is pretentious, as well. It does not reflect the way people speak. Grammarians have always accepted *you* as both singular and plural. Why not accept a singular "*they*" as well?

As of 2019 grammarians did. Such major style guides as the *Associated Press, Chicago Manual of Style, MLA* style manual, and *APA* style manual approve of using *they* as a singular pronoun. The APA (American Psychological Association) stated:

> Use of the singular "they" is endorsed as part of the APA Style because it is inclusive of all people and helps writers avoid making assumptions about gender. Although usage of the singular "they" was once discouraged in academic writing, many advocacy groups and publishers have accepted and endorsed it, including Merriam-Webster's Dictionary.

Writers use third-person pronouns to show they are writing as an outside observer writing about other people and things. This style is called **writing in the *third person***. Notice J. K. Rowling's use of third-person pronouns in this excerpt from *Harry Potter and the Sorcerer's Stone*. The pronouns show that the story teller is an outside observer, not part of the story.

> Something very painful was going on in Harry's mind. As Hagrid's story came to a close, **he** saw again the blinding flash of green light, more clearly than **he** had ever remembered **it** before — and **he** remembered something else, for the first

time in **his** life: a high, cold, cruel laugh.
Harry Potter and the Sorcerer's Stone by J. K.
Rowling

REFLEXIVE AND INTENSIVE PRONOUNS

Pronouns with the suffix *-self* or *-selves* are either *reflexive* or *intensive* pronouns. Both reflexive and intensive pronouns end in *-self* or *-selves*, but they have different uses. If they reflect back to a noun that has already been mentioned, they are **reflexive** pronouns. If they are used to put special emphasis on a noun or pronoun in the same sentence, they are **intensive pronouns**. They *intensify* the word's impact.

<u>*Reflexive*</u>

> **Alexa** taught **herself** how to skate.
> (*Herself* is a pronoun that reflects back to *Alexa* to avoid repetition of her name.)

<u>*Intensive*</u>:

I would rather do it **myself**.
(*Myself*" is used for emphasis. It could be eliminated and the sentence would still make sense.)

Below is a table of reflexive/intensive pronouns. (<u>NOTE</u>: There is no such word as *theirselves*.)

Personal Pronouns: Reflexive and Intensive		
	SINGULAR	**PLURAL**
FIRST PERSON	myself	ourselves
SECOND PERSON	yourself	yourselves
THIRD PERSON	himself, herself, itself	themselves

Don't use *-self* and *-selves* pronouns needlessly for *I, me, you,* and so on. In addition, do not use a *-self* or *-selves* pronoun to begin a sentence. (This makes sense because *-self* and *-selves* pronouns refer back to a noun or pronoun previously mentioned in the sentence.) Examples of correct and incorrect usage are given below.

<u>*Correct:*</u> My brother and I will go.
<u>*Incorrect:*</u> My brother and myself will go.

<u>*Correct*</u>: This is for you.
<u>*Incorrect*</u>: This is for yourself.

<u>*Correct*</u>: You and your friends should arrive before noon.
<u>*Incorrect*</u>: Yourself and your friends . . . or Your friends and yourself . . ..

<u>*Correct*</u>: The coach chose Joe and me.
<u>*Incorrect:*</u> The coach chose Joe and myself.

<u>Correct</u>: She gave the book to me.
<u>Incorrect</u>: She gave the book to myself.

RELATIVE PRONOUNS

Relative pronouns introduce a group of words that tell about a noun. They *relate,* or connect, the word-group to the noun. The most common relative pronouns are **who**, **which**, and **that**. See the table below for these and others.

COMMON RELATIVE PRONOUNS
who, whoever, whom, whomever, whose
which, whichever
what, whatever
that

The word group that begins with a relative pronoun is a *clause.* Since the word group tells about a noun, it is an *adjective clause.*

Notice that some relative pronouns, such as *who*, are the same as interrogative pronouns (which ask a question.) When used as relative pronouns, however, they do not ask a question or begin a sentence.

In addition, the relative pronoun *that* is the same as the demonstrative pronoun *that*. When used as a demonstrative pronoun, *that* points to something (e.g., *this* or *that*). When used as a relative pronoun, *that* introduces a clause and is followed by a verb.

DEMONSTRATIVE PRONOUNS

Demonstrative comes from a Latin word meaning "to point out," and in grammar, a demonstrative is a word that points out which person or thing is being referred to. English has demonstratives: *this, that, these and those.* **This** (singular) and **these** (plural) point to something that is **nearer** in distance or time. **That** (singular) and **those** (plural) point to something that is **farther** in distance or time.

> **Demonstrative Pronouns: *This; That***
> Which *puppy* is mine? *This* is mine. *That* is yours.

This, that, these, and *those* can be used either as demonstrative pronouns or demonstrative adjectives. In the example above, *this* and *that* are demonstrative pronouns. Why?

Remember that a pronoun is a word that replaces a noun that has already been mentioned (the pronoun's *antecedent.*) Pronouns come *after* their antecedents. In the example above, the antecedent of both *this* and *that* is "puppy." *This* and *that* come after "puppy," (their antecedent). Thus, they are pronouns.

An adjective, on the other hand, comes *before* the *noun* it refers to. It gives more information about that noun. Demonstrative adjectives answer the question *Which?* about a noun. (Chapter 4 discusses adjectives.) In the example that follows, *this* and *that* are used as adjectives. They come *before* the noun they refer to (*puppy*).

Demonstrative Adjectives: *This; That*

This puppy is staring at us.

That puppy is yawning.

INTERROGATIVE PRONOUNS

Interrogative pronouns ask questions. Think: "They interrogate." The interrogative pronouns are: ***Who? What? Which? Whose?*** and ***Whom?***

Interrogative pronouns ask questions that can be answered with a noun. For example: ***Who*** *won first prize?* (The answer is a noun, a person's name.) Notice that an interrogative pronoun is the *first word* in a question.

> ***Who*** is up first?
>
> ***What*** is the answer?
>
> ***Which*** twin is taller?
>
> ***Whose*** book is this?
>
> ***Whom*** did you meet? (This usage is correct, but not common. "*Who* did you meet?" is common usage, although strictly speaking, it is incorrect.)

INDEFINITE PRONOUNS

Indefinite pronouns, as their name suggests, do not refer to a definite person, place or thing. Instead, they refer to general, indefinite persons or things. See a list of indefinite pronouns in the table below.

Notice that some are singular, some are plural, and some can be either singular or plural, depending on what they refer to. For example, the pronoun *all* is singular in the phrase "*all* the *milk* is gone" because *all* refers to *milk,* which is singular. (It is thought of as one thing, not a number of things.)

COMMON INDEFINITE PROUNOUS		
SINGULAR		
another	everyone	nothing
anybody	everything	one
anyone	little	other
anything	much	somebody
each	neither	someone
either	nobody	something
everybody	no one	
PLURAL		
both	few	many
others	several	
SINGULAR OR PLURAL		
all	any	more
most	none	some

When *all* refers to one thing, it takes a singular verb: *is*. But in the phrase "*all* the *cookies* are gone" *all* is plural. It refers to a number of things: *cookies*.

Because indefinite pronouns do not replace nouns they do not have antecedents. Why are they called pronouns if they don't replace nouns? It's because they have the same uses in sentences as nouns. Just like a noun, an indefinite pronoun can be the subject of a sentence, the object, and so on.

SUBJECT AND OBJECT PRONOUNS

Personal pronouns have different forms to show how they are being used in a sentence. If the pronoun is performing the action in a sentence (or if it follows a linking verb) it is a *subject pronoun*. If the pronoun receives the action of the verb or follows a preposition, it is an *object pronoun*.

(Prepositions are explained in Chapter Six. They are words such as *to, for, from, over, under,* and *on*. A preposition shows the relationship between its noun and its verb.)

Subject pronouns are said to be in the *subjective case*. (Some grammar books call it the *nominative case*.) Object pronouns are said to be in the *objective case*. There are only five pronouns that change their form in the objective case. They are: *I, he, she, we,* and *they*. See the table.

Subject	Object
I	me
he	him
she	her
we	us
they	them

A common mistake is to use the wrong form of a pronoun in a sentence.

Incorrect:

Him and *me* ran a race.

Correct:

He and *I* ran a race.

Notice in the example that the verb is *ran.* To find the subject of *ran,* ask, *who ran?* The answer is *he* and *I.* Together, *he* and *I* are a compound subject. Both *he* and *I* are subject pronouns.

The following sentences begin with subject pronouns and end with pronouns that are objects of prepositions. Decide which of the choices in parentheses is correct.

1. They want you to go with Jim and (*me* or *I*).
2. He sat between (*him* and *her* or *he* and *she*).
3. She left George with (*he* or *him.*
4. We got a gift from (*they* or *them*).
5. I wrote letters to (*us* and *them* or *we* and *they.*

The correct sentences end with object pronouns:
1. They want to go with Jim and me.
2. He sat between him and her.
3. She left George with him.
4 We got a gift from them.
5. I wrote letters to us and them.

Name two
pronouns.
Who?
Me?

CHAPTER 2

PRONOUNS CHECK-UP

(Scroll down for answers.)

Pronouns and Antecedents

Choose the correct pronoun in parentheses and identify its antecedent.

1. School has (*his, its)* problems.
2. Each needs (*his, your)* own ticket.
3. All of the girls received (*their, her)* diplomas.
4. If anyone found a pen will (*he, they)* let me know.
5. People should be careful what (*she, they)* say.
6. The finance committee finished (*its, their)* report.
7. We brought (*our, their)* own lunch.
8. Some received (*her, their)* grades today.
9. Several finished (*his, their)* test.
10. The student received (*his, their)* grades.

Person and Number

For each italicized pronoun in the sentences below, give its *person* (1st, 2nd, or 3rd) and its *number* (singular or plural).

1. Sean, *you* need to leave now.
2. *We* will be in Egypt in March.
3. *They* told us to meet them here.
4. *I* write mystery novels.
5. *She* has brown eyes.
6. *It* really doesn't matter.
7. Mike gave the tickets to *us*.
8. Tom and Jeff, *you* are late.
9. Is this gift from *them?*
10. Did *he* write this?

Possessive Pronouns
Supply possessive pronouns for the blanks.

1. When you see someone grin, ___ face muscles
   automatically imitate a grin.
2. With the world's highest density of moose,
   Sweden can boast of ____ huge moose population.
3. Carrots get ____ color from carotene.
4. Sean, is this ____ notebook?
5. I drove to Gettysburg on ____ vacation.
6. Do we need ____ passports for this trip?
7. England's Elizabeth I was known for ____ keen
   political insights.
8. Since you came in first, this trophy is ____.

Reflexive and Intensive Pronouns
Choose the correct form of the pronoun.
1. Did the children paint this (*themselves,
   theirselves*)?
2. The secret is known only to you and (*me, myself*).
3. Lindsey and I completed the work (*ourself,
   ourselves*).
4. Jeanine did not write these words (*herself,
   themselves*).
5. I have never cared for snails (*myself, themselves*).
6. We'd rather do it (*ourself, ourselves*).
7. Amy, do you (*yourself, yourselves*) agree?
8. The music (itself, itselves) jarred our nerves.
9 Alli, did you write this (*yourself, yourselves*)?
10. Jack (*himself, hisself*) sings in the shower.
11. Shall we give the prize to (*them, themselves*)?
12. This dessert is for (*you, yourself*).

Relative Pronouns
Identify seven relative pronouns in the following
paragraph.

Edwin Hubbell was an astronomer who discovered that there are galaxies outside the Milky Way (which is in the Andromeda galaxy). It is Hubbell to whom we owe knowledge that more than 100 billion galaxies exist in the observable universe. Before Hubbell, astronomers were aware of only one galaxy that is in the universe, the galaxy which is our own.

Demonstrative Pronouns

Identify the italicized word as a demonstrative pronoun or a demonstrative adjective.

1. That incident? I am not concerned about *that*.
2. I need to change *this* password.
3. Don't give them the chocolate cookies. Give them *these*.
4. *Those* children caused the disturbance.
5. Do *this* now or you will regret it.
6. *This* answer is incorrect.
7. *That* is my house.
8. *That* plant needs to be watered.
9. The trees we pruned are pine trees. *Those* are cedars.
10. Don't open *that* gate.

Interrogative Pronouns

Identify the correct interrogative pronoun in each sentence.

1. *Who/Whom/What* left the door open?
2. *Which/Whose/What* is your opinion?
3. *Which/Whose/What* twin is taller?
4. *Who/Whom/Whose* notebook is this?
5. *Which/Who/Whom* left the door open?

Indefinite Pronouns
     Identify the indefinite pronoun and choose the verb that goes with it.

1. All the tickets *was/were* sold.
2. *Is/Are* any of the money missing?
3. Nobody in my family *live/lives* near me.
4. *Has/Have* each of the senators voted?
5. *Does/Do* either of you need money?
6. Few of the cookies *is/are* left.
7. Many of us *like/likes* classical music.
8. None of the members *is/are* absent.
9. Somebody in the audience *is/are* snoring.
10. Both of the trains *go/goes* to Boston.

Subject and Object Pronouns
     Correct the incorrect pronouns in each sentence. (NOTE: In some cases the correct pronouns might sound awkward because the phrasing is not commonly used.)

1. Him and me will go with you.
2. The teacher gave Wally and she a lecture.
3. I'm planning a vacation for you and I.
4. Us and them are not invited.
5. Keep this between you and I.
6 The candidate for who I voted lost the election.
7. I'm glad it was us who won.
8. Did her and them arrive yet?
9. Us and them were never there.
10. Did her or him write this?

CHAPTER 2

PRONOUNS: ANSWERS

Pronouns and Antecedents
1. its, School
2. his, Each
3. their, All
4. he, anyone
5. they, People
6. its, committee
7. our, We
8. their, Some
9. their, Several
10. his, Student

Person and Number
1. 2nd, singular
2. 1st, plural
3. 3rd, plural
4. 1st, singular
5. 3rd, singular
6. 3rd, singular
7. 1st, plural
8. 2nd, plural
9. 3rd, plural
10. 3rd, singular

Possessive Pronouns
1. your
2. its
3. their
4. your
5. my
6. our

7. her
8. yours

Reflexive and Intensive Pronouns
1. themselves
2. me
3. ourselves
4. herself
5. myself
6. ourselves
7. yourself
8. itself
9. yourself
10. himself
11. them
12. you

Relative Pronouns
1. who (*discovered*)
2. that (*there are*)
3. which (*is in the*)
4. whom (*we owe*
5. that (*more than*)
6. that (*is in the*)
7. which (*is our own*)

Demonstrative Pronouns
1. pronoun
2. adjective
3. pronoun
4. adjective
5. pronoun
6. adjective
7. adjective
8. adjective

9. pronoun
10. adjective

Interrogative Pronouns
1. Who
2. What
3. Which
4. Whose
5. Who

Indefinite Pronouns
1. All, were
2. any, Is
3. Nobody, lives
4. each, Has
5. either, Does
6. Few, are
7. Many, like
8. None, are
9. Somebody, is
10. Both, go

Subject and Object Pronouns
1. He and I
2. and her
3. you and me
4. We and they
5. you and me
6. for whom
7. was we
8. she and they
9. we and they
10. she or he

One of the glories of English
simplicity is the possibility of using
the same word as noun and verb.
— *Edward Sapir*

VERBS

A verb is a necessary part of every sentence. Verbs express action or link the subject of the sentence to the rest of the sentence. Verbs that express action are called *action verbs*. Verbs that link the subject of the sentence to the rest of the sentence are called *linking verbs* (also known as *state of being* verbs.)

A verb is the most important word in a sentence. Indeed, there can be no sentence without it. That verb can be an *action verb* (e.g., *jumps, sings*), or it can be a *linking verb* (e.g., *is, feels*). A linking verb joins a noun or pronoun to something that is said about it.

Action Verb:
Snakes **slither**.   They **slither**.

Linking Verb
Snakes **are** reptiles.   They **are** reptiles.

ACTION VERBS

A verb that expresses an action is called, appropriately, an **action verb**. That action may be a physical action (e.g., "sing") or a mental action (e.g., "think"). Here are some more examples. You can undoubtedly think of many others.

Physical actions:

bring, do, enter, give, write, go, hop, leave, send, sit, grab, listen, write, send, jog, say

Mental actions:

> agree, think, remember, listen, decide, believe, know, understand, consider

There are two different classifications of action verbs: (1) *transitive/ intransitive verbs*; and (2) *active/passive* verbs. These terms are explained below.

TRANSITIVE/INTRANSITIVE VERBS

A verb is *transitive* or *intransitive* depending on whether or not it has to have a *receiver* of its action in order to make sense.

Transitive Verbs

A verb that needs someone or something (an *object*) to make sense is called a **transitive verb**. *Transitive* comes from a Latin word meaning "carry over to." A *transitive verb* carries its action over to someone or something. It *transmits* its action to something else. For example, *bring* is a transitive verb. It needs an object to make sense.

> NOT A SENTENCE. They bring.
> (Bring who? Bring what?)

> SENTENCE: They bring gifts.
> (Bring what? Bring gifts. *Gifts* is the object of *bring*.)

A transitive verb carries its action from the subject of the sentence to the object. In the sentence "The batter hit the ball," the transitive verb *hit* carries the action from the subject, *batter*, over to the object, *ball*.

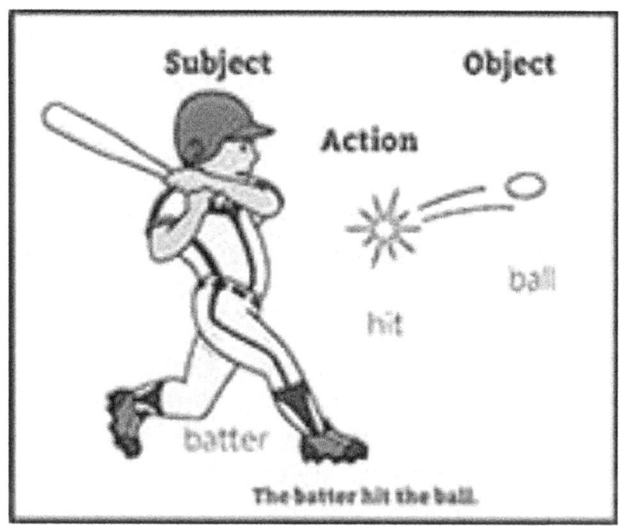

Here are some more examples of transitive verbs and their objects:

> The bride *cut* the *cake*.
> Jess *loves* psychological *thrillers*.
> He *carried* his *suitcase* upstairs.
> The spider *ate* a *fly*.
> She *caught* a *cold*.

Intransitive Verbs

A verb that does not require an object to complete its meaning is called an **intransitive verb**. The prefix *in* means "not," so that *intransitive* means "not transitive." An intransitive verb does not have an object. In the sentence, "Time flies," the verb *flies* is intransitive because no object is required to complete its meaning. "Time flies,'" makes sense and is a sentence. Most verbs can be either transitive or intransitive. For example, if we say, "The pianist *played* a concerto," *played* is transitive; but if we say, "The pianist *played*," *played* is intransitive.

LINKING VERBS

TO RECAP: There are two main classes of verbs: **action verbs** and **linking verbs**. Action verbs express actions – physical or mental.

What about **linking verbs?** Linking verbs do not express actions. Instead, they *link* nouns or pronouns to words that define or describe them. Notice the link in the sentence below.

Trout **are** fish.

In the sentence, *"Trout are fish,"* the verb is *are*. "*Are* obviously is not an action verb; it is a verb linking *trout* to *fish*. "Fish" is a word that describes "trout." In fact, it names what *trout* are: *fish*.

Think of a linking verb as an equals sign or a scales. Whatever is on one side is equal to whatever is on the other side: *trout = fish*.

THE VERB *BE*

Be as a Linking Verb

The most common linking verb is the verb *be*. It is the most important verb in English. We use it all the time and in all its forms. The verb *be* has eight forms — more than any other verb in English. They are: ***be. am, is, are, was, were, being, been***. The verb *be* indicates existence — being. It indicates that someone or something *is*: it exists. *Be* is often referred to as a "state of being" verb.

The following tables show the forms to use for the tenses of the *be* verb. (*Tense* means the time of the verb; whether it is in the present, past, or future, for example. *Tense* is explained in more detail later on in this chapter.)

The Verb "be," Present Tense		
	Singular	Plural
1st Person	I **am**	we **are**
2nd Person	you **are**	you **are**
3rd Person	he **is** she **is** it **is**	they **are**

The Verb "be," Past Tense		
	Singular	**Plural**
1st Person	I **was**	we **were**
2nd Person	you **were**	you **were**
3rd Person	he **was** she **was** it **was**	they **were**

The Verb "be," Future Tense		
	Singular	**Plural**
1st person	I **will be**	we **will be**
2nd person	you **will be**	you **will be**
3rd person	he **will be** she **will be** it **will be**	they **will be**
NOTE: In very formal English, *shall* may be used instead of *will* for 1st person, future tense. *Shall* is also used in questions: "*Shall* we go?"		

Verb Phrases

The verb **be** is not always a single word. Often it is combined with "helping verbs " to make a verb of two or more words. A verb made up of two or more words is called a **verb phase.** For example, the verb phrase *will be* is made from the main verb, *be,* plus the helping verb *will. Will be* indicates something that *will be* (or will exist) in the future. For example: "Tomorrow ***will be*** Friday."

The chart below shows verb phrases for the verb **be.** The main verb is in bold and the helping verbs are in italics.

shall **be**	*has* **been**
will **be**	*have* **been**
can **be**	*had* **been**
might **be**	*might have* **been**
may **be**	*may have* **been**
must **be**	*must have* **been**
could **be**	*could have* **been**
shall **be**	*shall have* **been**
should **be**	*should have* **been**
would **be**	*will have* **been**

NOTE: The verb *be* is not always a linking verb. It can be used as a "helping verb" to help form verb tenses.

OTHER COMMON LINKING VERBS

Be is not the only linking verb. There are many others. They include verbs for the senses: *sight, hearing, smelling, tasting,* and *feeling.* Notice in the following examples that common linking verbs can be replaced by forms of the verb *be.*

He *looks tired.*
He *is* tired.

The water *felt* icy.
The water *was* icy.

That chili will *taste* spicy.
That chili will *be* spicy.

Other common linking verbs include:
*act, appear, become, come, get, grow,
indicate, prove, remain, seem, stay, turn*

Examples:

She *acts* confident.
The audience *appears* restless.

Verbs that Can Be Either Action or Linking

Some verbs can be either action verbs or linking verb. They include:
*act, appear, become, feel, get, grow, look,
prove, remain, seem, smell, sound, turn,
stay, taste*

Examples:

The dog *smells* a bone. (action verb)
That dessert *smells* delicious! (linking verb.

They *grow* impatient. (linking verb).
The weeds *grow* quickly. (action verb)

SUMMARY: Action verbs show what someone or something **does.** Linking verbs show what someone or something **is.**

THE PRINCIPAL PARTS OF VERBS

A verb has four main forms, called **principal parts**. These are used to show the verb's **tense**, or time (e.g., whether the verb's action is in the past, present, or future.)

The four principal parts, or forms, of a verb are:

1. present

2. present participle

3. past

4. past participle.

The table below shows the four principal parts of the verbs *ask, use,* and *move.*

PRINCIPAL PARTS OF VERBS			
Present	**Present Participle**	**Past**	**Past Participle**
ask	(am) asking	asked	(have) asked
use	(am) using	used	(have) used
move	(am) moving	moved	(have) moved

PARTICIPLES AND HELPING VERBS

The first principal part, the *present*, is the base form of the verb. It is the verb part listed in the dictionary. The *present participle* and *past participle* must be combined with a helping verb to be used in a sentence. Since they (together with their helping verbs) are two or more words, they are called *verb phrases.* Examples of verb phrases include: *am asking, have asked, are using,* and *had used.* The examples below show these verb phrases used in sentences.

> *Examples:*
>
> I *ask* a question. (*present*)
> I *am asking* a question. (*present participle*)
> I *asked* a question. (*past*)
> I *have asked* a question. (*past participle*)
>
> Factories *use* robots. (*present*)
> Factories *are using* robots. (*present participle*)
> Factories *used* robots. (*past*)
> Factories *had used* robots. (*past participle*)

HELPING (AUXILIARY) VERBS

You have seen that the past participles and present participles of verbs are used with *helping verbs,* such as *am, are, has, had* (also called *auxiliary verbs*). Helping verbs help a verb express tense. For example, instead of merely the present, past, and future, helping verbs enable verbs to express an action that *continues* in the present, past, or future – or an action that *could occur* in the present, past, or future.

The Verb *be* As a Helping Verb

You know that as a linking verb, *be* connects a noun or pronoun with a word or words that name or describe it: e.g., "Dogs are canines." But the verb *be* can also be used as a helping verb to help a main verb form tenses. *Be* is used as a helping verb with the present participle form of a verb – the *-ing* form of the verb: e.g., "The train *is leaving* the station."

It is easy to tell if the *be* verb is being used as a linking verb or as a helping verb. If a noun or pronoun comes before it and words that describe the noun or pronoun come after it, it is a *linking verb*. If it is used before the *-ing* form (present participle) of a verb, it is a *helping* (or *auxiliary verb*.

REGULAR VERBS

Most of the thousands of verbs in the English language are **regular verbs**. That is, they form the *past* and *past participle* forms in a regular manner:

    1. By adding *-ed* to the *present* form.

    2. Or, by adding *-d* to the *present* form (if the present form already ends in *e*).

Since regular verbs follow the same pattern, they do not need to be memorized; but here are a few for you to note their pattern. Try saying them out loud.

PRINCIPAL PARTS OF REGULAR VERBS			
Present	Present Participle	Past	Past Participle
walk	(am) walking	walked	(have) walked
talk	(am) talking	talked	(have) talked
jump	(am) jumping	jumped	(have) jumped
change	(am) changing	changed	(have) changed
cook	(am) cooking	cooked	(have) cooked
laugh	(am) laughing	laughed	(have) laughed
arrive	(am) arriving	arrived	(have) arrived

IRREGULAR VERBS

Most verbs are regular. Some of the most common verbs, however, are **irregular**. That is, they do *not* form their past and past participles the regular way, by adding *-ed* or *-d* to the present. Instead, they form their *past* and *past participles* in a variety of ways:

(1) by changing the vowel
(2) by changing consonants
(3) by adding *-en*
(4) by using the same form for all principal parts

(What about the *present participle* of irregular verbs? Fortunately, the present participles of irregular verbs are regular. That is, they always form the present participle the same way: by adding *-ing* to the present.)

Since irregular verbs do not follow the "rules," it is easy to make mistakes by using the wrong forms. This makes it necessary to learn the principal parts for every irregular verb. Does this seem overwhelming? Since there are only about two hundred irregular verbs (and you probably don't use all two hundred regularly), the task is feasible. As you study the irregular verbs listed below, keep in mind that the past participle is *never* used alone. That is why it is incorrect to say, "I *begun*," but it is correct to say, "I *have begun*." On the other hand, the past form is *never* used with *have, has,* or *had.* That is why it is incorrect to say, "I have *began.*"

As you study irregular verbs, it may be helpful to say or think, "have" before the past participle. (You only need to learn three principal parts because the present participle always ends in *-ing.*)

In order to make your study of irregular verbs
more manageable, the list of irregular verbs is
divided into four smaller groups. beginning with
simpler verbs and continuing with verbs frequently
misused and those that need special attention.

GROUP 1: IRREGULAR VERBS

Present (Today I)	Past (Yesterday I)	Past Participle (I have)
1. beat	beat	beaten
2. begin	began	begun
3. blow	blew	blown
4. break	broke	broken
5. bring	brought	brought
6. burst	burst	burst
7. come	came	come

Notes on Verbs in Group 1:
1. **Beat.** Do not use *beat* with *have, has,* or *had.*
2. **Begin.** Do not use *begun* alone. *Begun* is used with *have, has,* or *had.*
3. **Blow.** There is no verb form *"blowed."*
4. **Break.** Never use *broke* with *have, has,* or *had.*
5. **Bring.** Notice that *brought* is used for both the past and past participle. There is no word *"brang"* or *"brung."*
6. **Burst.** Notice that there is only one verb form for the verb *burst.* There is no verb *"bust,"* *"busted,"* or *"bursted."*

7. **Come.** *Come* should never be used when you are referring to the past. *Came* should never be used with *have, has,* or *had.* Don't say, "He *come* over yesterday," or, "Has he *came* over yet?" The correct forms are: "He *came* over yesterday," and "Has he *come* over yet?"

GROUP 2: IRREGULAR VERBS		
Present (Today I)	**Past** (Yesterday I)	**Past Participle** (I have)
1. do	did	done
2. draw	drew	draw
3. drink	drank	drunk
4. eat	ate	eaten
5. flee	fled	fled
6. fly	flew	flown
7. flow	flowed	flowed

Notes on Verbs in Group 2:
1. **Do.** *Done* must never be used when referring to the past. Instead of, "Who *done* it?" say, "Who *did* it?" or, "Who has *done* it?"

2. **Draw.** There is no such verb as *drawed.*

3. **Drink.** Many of the mistakes made in connection with this verb is because the word *drunk* has an unpleasant connotation. But *drunk* is the past participle of *drink,* and no other form should be used with *have, has,* and *had.* The sentence, "I have *drunk* a glass of water," is correct.

84

5-7. **Flee, fly, flow.** The three verbs *flee, fly,* and *flow* are often confused. Remember that *flown* is the past participle of the irregular verb *fly*. It has nothing to do with *flow*.

GROUP 3: IRREGULAR VERBS		
Present (Today I)	**Past** (Yesterday I)	**Past Participle** (I have)
1. go	went	gone
2. grow	grew	grown
3. hang	hung	hung
4. ring	rang	rung
5. swim	swam	swum
6. swing	swung	swung
7. write	wrote	written

Notes on Verbs in Group 3:

1. **Go.** Remember that the past form, *went,* is always used alone.

   Incorrect: have went, has went, had went

2. **Grow.** There is no verb "*growed.*"

3. **Hang.** There are two verbs *hang.* The irregular verb (shown in the list) is used in speaking of things: e.g., "I *hung* a picture" and "My coat *has hung* in the closet for months." The regular verb *hang* is used only in reference to executing persons: e.g., "The murderer was *hanged.*"

4. **Ring.** The past form, *rang,* is never used with *have, has,* or *had.*

Incorrect: "*Has* the bell *rang?*"

5. **Swim.** The past tense, *swam,* must never be used with *have, has,* or *had.*

   Incorrect: "I *have swam* in the ocean."

6. **Swing.** Notice that the forms for the *past* and *past participle* are the same. There is no word "*swang.*"

7. **Write.** Don't use have, has, or had with wrote.

Incorrect: I *haven't wrote* to him yet.

Correct: I *haven't written* to him yet.

GROUP 4: IRREGULAR VERBS		
Present (Today I)	**Past** (Yesterday I)	**Past Participle** (I have)
1. cast	cast	cast
2. broadcast	broadcast	broadcast
3. throw	threw	thrown
4. fall	fell	fallen
5. freeze	froze	frozen
6. run	ran	run
7. see	saw	seen
8. sing	sang	sung
9. speak	spoke	spoken
10. steal	stole	stolen

Notes on Verbs in Group 4:

1. **Cast.** Notice that all three forms of the verb are the same. There is no word "casted."

86

2. **Broadcast.** Like "cast," all three forms of the verb are the same.

3. **Throw.** There are no words "*throwed*" and "*thrun.*"

4. **Fall.** The past form, *fell*, must never be used with *have, has,* or *had.*

   Incorrect: I *haven't fell* off a ladder yet.
   Correct: I *haven't fallen* off a ladder yet.

5. **Freeze.** The past form, *froze,* should never be used with *have, has,* or *had.*

6. **Run.** It is incorrect to say, "I *run* a mile yesterday." Rather, say, "I *ran* a mile yesterday."

7. **Saw.** The past and past participle are often confused. We hear, "I have *saw* him," and, "I *seen* him." Both of these are incorrect. *Saw* must never be used with *have, has,* or *had,* and *seen* must never be used without *have, has,* or *had.* "I *saw* him," and, "I have *seen* him" are correct.

8. **Sing.** The past form is *sang,* not *sung.* "I *sang* a song yesterday" is correct, not, "I *sung* a song yesterday."

9. **Speak.** Do not use *spoke* with *have, has,* or *had.* Say, "Have you *spoken* to him about it?" not," Have you *spoke* to him about it?"

10. **Steal.** Do not use *have, has,* or *had* with *stole.*

Common Error
With Irregular Verbs

A common error with irregular verbs is to form the past tense the same way as with regular verbs – by adding **-ed**.

Incorrect: throwed, knowed, bursted, stealed

Correct: threw, knew, burst, stole

CHARACTERISTICS OF VERBS

TO RECAP: Verbs are unique. They are the only words in a sentence that can show action or a "state of being." Moreover, a sentence cannot be a sentence without a verb.

Verbs have five characteristics that distinguish them. They are:

1. **Person** (1st person, 2nd person, 3rd person)
2. **Number** (singular or plural)
3. **Tense** (time of the action or state)
4. **Voice** (active or passive)
5. **Mood** (fact, command, or conditional)

PERSON

Third-Person Singular, Present Tense

In Chapter 2, you learned that pronouns have special forms to show 1st person, 2nd person, and 3rd person. Verbs also have person, but most verbs do not change their form to show person, *except* in the following case:

If the subject of the verb is *3rd-person singular* (e.g., *he, she, it*) . . . and *if* the *time* of the verb is the *present* . . . **then** add *-s* or *-es* to the verb.

See the following table for the action verb *play*. Notice that in the present tense, *play* does not change its form *except* for the 3rd-person singular, which adds the *-s* ending.

In the past tense, *played* does not change its form at all. The forms for 1st, 2nd, and 3rd persons remain the same: *played*.

	Present Tense	
	Singular	**Plural**
1st Person	I *play*	we *play*
2nd Person	you play	you *play*
3rd Person	he (she, it) plays	they *play*

	Past Tense	
	Singular	**Plural**
1st Person	I *played*	we *played*
2nd Person	you *played*	you *played*
3rd Person	he (she, it) *played*	they *played*

Forms for Person:
Linking Verb *be*

The linking verb *be* is a unique case. It *does* have different forms for the 1st, 2nd, and 3rd person in both the present and the past. See the tables below.

The Verb "be," Present Tense		
	Singular	Plural
1st Person	I am	we are
2nd Person	you are	you are
3rd Person	he is she is it is	they are

The Verb "be," Past Tense		
	Singular	Plural
1st Person	I was	we were
2nd Person	you were	you were
3rd Person	he was she was it was	they were

<table>
<tr><th colspan="3">The Verb "be," Future Tense</th></tr>
<tr><td></td><td>Singular</td><td>Plural</td></tr>
<tr><td>1st person</td><td>I will be</td><td>we will be</td></tr>
<tr><td>2nd person</td><td>you will be</td><td>you will be</td></tr>
<tr><td>3rd person</td><td>he will be
she will be
it will be</td><td>they will be</td></tr>
<tr><td colspan="3">NOTE: In very formal English, shall may be used instead of will for 1st person, future tense. Shall is also used in questions: "Shall we go?"</td></tr>
</table>

NUMBER

In grammar, the word *number* means *singular and plural.* Verbs, like nouns and pronouns, have *number* — singular and plural forms. For a sentence to be grammatically correct, the subject (noun or pronoun) and its verb must agree with one another in *number.* That is, if the subject is singular, the verb must be singular; if the subject is plural, the verb must be plural.

This seems logical. Yet it can be tricky. Nouns usually add **-s** for the *plural.* Verbs in the present tense often do the opposite. Most 3rd-person singular verbs add **-s** for the *singular.*

Example:

The *student* yawn**s**. (singular)
The *student***s** yawn. (plural)

Notice that the first example sentence has a singular subject (*student*) and a singular verb (*yawns*). The

91

singular subject does *not* end in -*s*; the singular verb, however, does end in -*s*. The second example sentence has a plural subject (*students*) and a plural verb (*yawn*). The plural subject ends in -*s*: the plural verb does *not*.

Common error: Since you add -*s* to a noun to make it plural, a logical mistake is to add -*s* to a verb to make it plural.

Example:

> *Incorrect:* The student**s** *yawn**s***.
> *Correct:* The student**s** *yawn*.

To avoid this mistake: First, identify the subject of the sentence (the person or thing doing the action). Then identify the verb (the action word). If the subject is singular, the verb describing its action should be singular (ending in -*s*). If the subject is plural, the verb should be plural (no -*s*).

TENSE: THE TIME OF A VERB

Verbs are the only part of speech that show time — present, past, or future. The time of a verb is called its *tense* (from the Latin word *tempus*, meaning "time"). Verbs have three kinds of tenses:

(1) *simple* tenses

(2) *perfect* tenses

(3) *progressive* tenses

Simple Tenses

There are three simple tenses: (1) *present tense*, (2) *past tense*, and (3) *future tense*. These simply represent *present time*, *past time*, and *future time*. The sentences below illustrate the simple tenses, using the verb *drive:*

1. I usually *drive* to the beach. *(present tense)*

2. Yesterday they *drove* thirty miles. *(past tense)*

3. I *will drive* to Philadelphia tomorrow. *(future tense)*

The following table lists verb forms for the simple tenses:

SIMPLE TENSES		
PRESENT TENSE		
	Singular	**Plural**
1st person	I drive	we drive
2nd person	you drive	you drive
3rd person	(he, she, it) drives	they drive
PAST TENSE		
	Singular	**Plural**
1st person	I drove	we drove
2nd person	you drove	you drove
3rd person	(he, she, it) drove	they drove
FUTURE TENSE		
	Singular	**Plural**
1st person	I will drive	we will drive
2nd person	you will drive	you will drive
3rd person	(he, she, it) will drive	they will drive

Perfect Tenses

The term *perfect tenses* is a little misleading because it doesn't refer to tenses that have no mistakes. Instead, it means "completed." When you want to tell about something that is completed, or something that will be completed at a certain time in the future, use the *perfect* (completed) *tenses*.

Present Perfect Tense. The present perfect tense is formed by using *have* or *has*, followed by the *past participle* of the verb: e.g., "I *have laughed.*"

The present perfect is used in two ways:

1. For an action completed sometime in the past that is still continuing in the present.

    Example: "I *have lived* here all my life."
    (I began living here in the past and am still living here.)

2. For an action that happened in the past, but at some indefinite time. In other words, the time at which an action occurred is not specified.

    Example: "We *have talked* before."
    (We have talked in the past, but exactly when in the past is not stated. It is either unknown or unimportant.)

3. To describe an action that never happened.

    Example: "I *have never* lived in Brazil.*"
    (I never lived in Brazil in the past, and I still do not live in Brazil.)

Common error. A common error is to confuse the simple past and present perfect. If an action was completed *at a specific time in the past,* use the simple past.

    Example: "I *did* my homework last night."

    ("Last night" is a specific time, so the verb is simple past: *did.*)

    Example: "I *have done* my homework."

    (No specific time in the past is specified, so the verb is in the present perfect: *have done.*)

Past Perfect Tense. The past perfect tense is formed by *had* followed by the past participle of the verb: e.g., "She *had driven* three miles before she heard the siren." Notice that there are two past-tense verbs in that sentence. *Had driven* is in the past perfect tense because it happened *before* another action in the past — *heard.*

The *past perfect tense* is used to show that one action in the past was completed *before* another action in the more recent past. For example, in the sentence "I *had finished* before the bell *rang,*" the action *had finished* (past perfect) was completed before the action *rang* (simple past).

Future Perfect Tense. The future perfect tense is formed by *will have* followed by the past participle of the verb: e.g., "She *will have driven* two thousand miles." The future perfect tense is used to show that an action in the future will be completed *before* another action in the future: e.g., "Our plane *will have left* before we *reach* the airport."

The table below shows perfect tense forms for the verb *drive.*

PERFECT TENSES	
Singular	Plural
Present Perfect Tense	
I have driven	we have driven
you have driven	you have driven
(he, she, it) has driven	they have driven
Past Perfect Tense	
I had driven	we had driven
you had driven	you had driven
(he, she, it) had driven	they had driven
Future Perfect Tense	
I will have driven	we will have driven
you will have driven	you will have driven
(he, she, it) will have driven	they will have driven

Progressive Tenses

Progressive tenses are used to show actions *in progress* – actions that continue.

The **present progressive** indicates an action that began in the present and is still going on: (e.g., "The snow *is melting* slowly.").

The **past progressive** indicates an action that began in the past and continued: (e.g., "The rain *was falling* steadily.")

The **future progressive** indicates an action that will begin in the future and will continue: (e.g., "Friday the storm *will be threatening* the coast.").

The table below lists verb forms of the progressive tenses for the verb *drive*.

Progressive Tenses	
Singular	**Plural**
Present Progressive Tense	
I am driving	we are driving
you are driving	you are driving
it is driving	they are driving
Past Progressive Tense	
I was driving	we were driving
you were driving	you were driving
it was driving	they were driving
Future Progressive Tense	
I will (shall) be driving	we will (shall) be driving
you will be driving	you will be driving
it will be driving	they will be driving
Present Perfect Progressive Tense	
I have been driving	we have been driving
you have been driving	you have been driving
it has been driving	they have been driving
Past Perfect Progressive Tense	
I had been driving	we had been driving
you had been driving	you had been driving
it had been driving	they had been driving
Past Perfect Progressive Tense	
I will (shall) have been driving	we shall (will) have been driving
you will have been driving	you will have been driving
it will have been driving	they will have been driving

Present Progressive. The *present progressive tense* shows action in the present that is continuing; it is going on now. The present progressive is formed by using *is* or *are* with the *-ing* form of the verb (the present participle).
    Example: The snow *is melting* slowly.

Past Progressive. The *past progressive tense* shows action in the past that continued. It is formed by using *was* or *were* with the *-ing* form of the verb (the present participle).
    Example: The rain *was falling* steadily.

Future Progressive. The *future progressive tense* shows action that will begin in the future and will continue. It is formed by using *will be* with the *-ing* form of the verb (the present participle).
    Example: The hurricane *will be threatening* the East Coast.

Present Perfect Progressive. The *present perfect progressive tense* shows a continuous action that began in the past and continues in the present. It is formed by using *has been* or *have been* with the *-ing* form of the verb (the present participle).
    Example: I *have been practicing* yoga regularly since February.

Past Perfect Progressive. *The past perfect progressive tense* shows an action that began in the past, continued in the past, and *ended* at a specific time in the past. It is formed by using *had been* with the *-ing* form of the verb (the present participle). The words *before, for,* or *since* are often used near a verb in the *past perfect progressive tense.*

> *Example:* We *had been walking* for two miles before we realized we were on the wrong road.

Future Perfect Progressive. The *future perfect progressive tense* is used for an action that is expected to be continuing in the future It is formed by using *will have been* with the *-ing* form of the verb (the present participle).
Example:

> By the time I reach Arizona I will have been traveling for 48 hours.

VOICE: ACTIVE AND PASSIVE

Three characteristics of verbs are *person* (1st, 2nd, 3rd), *number* (singular, plural), and *tense* (time). Some active verbs have a 4rd characteristic: *voice* (active and passive). What does this mean?

When the subject of the sentence performs the action, the verb is in the *active voice.* But when the subject is being acted upon, the verb is in the *passive voice.*

Active Voice:

> The robin *ate* the worm.
>
> (The subject, *robin,* performs the action: *ate.)*

Passive Voice:

> The worm *was eaten* by the robin.
>
> (The subject, *worm,* is acted upon: *was eaten.)*

Creating the Passive

The passive forms of a verb are formed by combining a form of the *be* verb with the *past participle* of the main verb. Other helping verbs, such as *could*, are also sometimes present.

> *Example:* The steak *could have been eaten* by our Rottweiler.

The table illustrates how to form different tenses for the passive sentences *The bill is paid/ The bills are paid* using forms of the *be* verb with *paid* (the past participle of *pay*).

		Singular	Plural	Past Participle
Present	The bill/bills	is	are	paid
Present perfect	The bill/bills	has been	have been	paid
Past	The bill/bills	was	were	paid
Past perfect	The bill/bills	had been	had ben	paid
Future	The bill/bills	will be	will be	paid
Future perfect	The bill/bills	will have ben	will have been	paid
Present progressive	The bill/bills	is being	are being	paid
Past progressive	The bill/bills	was being	were being	paid

MOOD: INDICATIVE, IMPERATIVE SUBJUNCTIVE

So far, you found that verbs have *person* (1st, 2nd, 3rd), *number* (singular, plural), *tense* (time), and *voice* (active, passive). The final characteristic of verbs is **mood.** As with many terms in grammar, the term *mood* has a special meaning that has nothing to do with its ordinary meaning ("mood: a state of mind or emotion"). In grammar, *mood* refers to a feature of verbs that signals whether a sentence expresses:

1. A statement or question of fact

2. A command

3. An expression of doubt, uncertainty; a wish; a condition that is improbable or contrary to fact

For example, notice the difference in mood of the verbs in the following sentences.

-1. Those bills **are** paid. (*factual*)

2. **Pay** those bills! (*command*)

3. If only those bills **were paid**. (*wish; condition contrary to fact*. The fact is, the bills were not paid.)

The grammatical terminology for those three main moods of verbs are: (1) **Indicative Mood** (factual**); (2) Imperative Mood** (command); **(3) Subjunctive Mood**(wish, doubt, or condition contrary to fact).

Indicative Mood

Most sentences are written in the *indicative mood*. This is the factual mood. It *indicates* something. The indicative mood states a fact, asks about a fact, or denies a fact. The indicative mood can also express an opinion if the opinion is stated as if it were a fact. (In other words, not all statements of fact are necessarily true.)

The indicative mood is easy to identify. If a sentence is stated as a fact or asks a factual question, it is in the indicative mood. Some grammar books classify questions in a separate category called the *interrogative mood*. (Think of "to interrogate," to ask questions.) In English, the form of the verb does not change for questions. It is the word order in the sentence that changes.

The examples below are sentences in the *indicative* mood. They include statements of fact, opinions stated as facts, and factual questions.

Statements of Fact:

We had two inches of rain yesterday.
These apples were grown without pesticides.

Opinions Stated as Fact:

Undoubtedly it will rain tomorrow.
Granny Smith apples make the best pies.

Factual Questions:

What is the annual rainfall in Honolulu?
Where did you buy those apples?

Imperative Mood

The imperative mood is a command or request. The subject of an imperative sentence is the pronoun *you,* but the word *you* is usually understood and not stated.

Examples:

(*You*) Take the dog for a walk.
(*You*) Remember to lock the door.

The name of the person being spoken to may be included in an imperative sentence. The name is set-off from the rest of the sentence with commas. It may seem that the person's name is the subject of the sentence, but it is not. The subject is still the pronoun *you,* even if it is not stated.

Examples:

George, (*you*) have a good day
(*You*) Listen to the teacher, Jimmy.

Subjunctive Mood

The subjunctive mood expresses something that is not actual, but imaginary or wished for, whether or not it is possible. We use the subjunctive to talk about events that may or may not happen – events that someone wishes, anticipates, or imagines will happen. For example, "I wish I *were* (not *was*) lucky."

Other uses of the subjunctive are rare except in formal English. The following examples illustrate the use of the subjunctive in formal English:

1. The subjunctive is used in a clause beginning with *that* after a verb that means "to suggest, to advise."

   Example:

   I suggest *that* you *be* (not *are*) on time.

2. The subjunctive is used in a clause beginning with *that* after an adjective that means "advisable" or "anxious."

   Example:

   It is advisable *that* he *rest* (not *rests*).

The form of subjunctive verbs. The form of verbs in the subjunctive is quite simple. It is the base form of the verb – that is, the verb with no added endings or changed vowel sounds: e.g., *sing,* not *sings*. Note that the subjunctive verb does not change or add endings for person (*I, you, he,* etc.).

Examples of verbs in the subjunctive:

1. I wish she *were* here.

2. He recommends that we *arrive* early.

3. She suggested that we *meet* at the restaurant.

Subjunctive of the verb *be*. Use of the subjunctive mood is gradually fading out in English. Among English speakers the only problem likely to occur is use of the subjunctive of the verb *be*. The subjunctive form of a verb is its base form. What is the base form of *be?* In the present tense, the base form is *be* (not *is, am,* or *are*). In the past tense, the base form of *be* is *were* (not *was*).

Today the present subjunctive of *be* is seldom used. It persists in such expressions as, "If this *be* (not *is*) true . . ." indicating a condition that is uncertain or contrary to fact.

Example:

> "It this *be* (not *is*) treason, make the most of it." – *Patrick Henry*

Common error with *be*. It is the past subjunctive of *be* that is tricky. The past subjunctive of *be* is always *were*, not *was*. Thus, such commonly heard expressions as "I wish I *was* . . ." or "If only it *was* . . ." are grammatically incorrect. They should be: "I wish I *were* . . ." and "If only it *were* . . ." The subjunctive form of *be* should be used to indicate a condition that is uncertain or contrary to fact.

English, however is a growing language, constantly changing. Today such expressions as "I wish I *was*" are used so frequently, and by respected speakers of English, that they are seldom objected to. Remember, however, that on occasions where "correct English" is required, use "I wish I *were,*" not I wish I *was.*"

Here are some examples of when to use *was* and *were*. Each sentence in the Indicative group expresses a fact. Each sentence in the Subjunctive group expresses a condition that is uncertain or contrary to fact.

Indicative:

1. If he *was* there, why didn't he admit it? (He was there.)
2. If it *was* snowing, you should have stayed home. (It was snowing.)
3. If she *was* sick, why didn't she say so? (She was sick.)

Subjunctive:

1. If I *were* you, I would go. (I am not you.)
2. If James *were* here, he would help. (James is not here.)
3. If she *were* well, she would compete. (She is not well.)

GHOST to SCROOGE: I am the ghost of Christmas future perfect subjunctive. I will show you what would have happened to you, were you have changed your ways.

VERBALS:
GERUNDS, PARTICIPLES,
INFINITIVES

> *Verbals* are words formed from verbs that function as other parts of speech. There are three kinds of verbals: *gerunds*, *participles*, and *infinitives*.

TO RECAP: Earlier in this chapter you learned that verbs have four principal parts: (1) *present*, (2) *past*, (3) *present participle*, and (4) *past participle*. The principal parts are used to form the various tenses.

- The *present* and *past* principal parts form the simple tenses—*present* and *past*.
- The *present participle* and *past participle* are used with helping verbs to form the *perfect* and *progressive tenses*.

Verbals. Participles used by themselves, <u>withou</u>t helping verbs, are *verbals* – words formed from verbs that function as nouns, adjective, or adverbs. For example, *swimming* is the present particle of the verb *to swim*. It can be used by itself, however, as a noun: "Swimming is a great sport."

GERUNDS: VERBAL NOUNS

Gerunds are nouns formed from the present participle of verbs used by themselves. (The present participle is the verb form ending in *-ing*.) Although gerunds are formed from verbs, they function as nouns. They always end in *-ing*.

Examples:

> *Swimming* is an Olympic sport.
> I couldn't stop *laughing*.
> The dog's *barking* grew louder.

PARTICIPLES: VERBAL ADJECTIVES

Participles as adjectives. A past participle without a helping verb is a *verbal*. It does not function as an action verb. Instead, it functions as an *adjective* and modifies a noun.

Example:

> He *cut* the onions for the salad. (*verb*)
> He added *cut* onions to the salad. (*adjective*)

TO RECAP: The *past participle* of regular verbs is formed by adding *-ed* to the base form. For example, the past participle of *arrive* is *arrived*. The past participle of *irregular* verbs may have such endings as *-en, -t, -d,* or *-n.* Examples include: *break/broken, burn/burnt.* Some irregular verbs have past participles that are the same as their base forms: e.g., *burst/burst, cut/cut.*

INFINITIVES

An infinitive is the simplest form of a verb preceded by the word *to.*

Examples: to talk, to write, to be.

Although an infinitive is formed from a verb, it is a verbal. That is, it functions as another part of speech. Infinitives are used as nouns, as adjectives (to mdify nouns), or as adverbs (to modify verbs).

Examples:

1. *To err* is human (noun).
2. I lack the will power *to resist.* (adjective, modifying *will power*)
3. I use an antiseptic *to kill* germs. (adverb, modifying *use*)

Common "error" with infinitives. A common error in using infinitives is known as the **split infinitive.** This error is simple inserting a word or words between the word "to" and the infinitive verb." One of the better-known examples of this "error" is the Star Trek motto: "To **boldly** go where no one has gone before."

Grammarians in Victorian England decided that the split infinitive is an error. Today, however, the split infinitive is increasing in general usage and acceptance.

*

WORD HISTORY

Gerund: The word *gerund* comes from the Latin *gerundium*, meaning "to be carried out." It is called this because 18th-century grammarians, the gerund expressed "the doing or the necessity of doing something.

Infinitive: The word *infinitive* come from the Latin *infinitivus*, meaning "unlimited, indefinite." The infinitive is "indefinite" in the sense that it is a simple verb form that has no person, number, or tense. It is simply "to" plus the base form of the verb. An infinitive is what is termed in grammar, a "*non-finite verb*, meaning, "a verb that does not show tense." A non-finite verb cannot be the main verb in a sentence because the main verb must indicate the time of the action (tense). Thus, an infinitive cannot be the main verb in a sentence.

CHAPTER 3.

VERBS: CHECK-UP

(Scroll down for answers.)

Action and Linking Verbs
Identify each verb in the following sentences and decide if it is an action verb or linking verb.

1. The average blue whale's heart is the size of a car.
2. In 1770 the British Parliament banned lipstick, because it was "a weapon of witchcraft."
3. We left before the road grew icy.
4. In 1983 in Scotland, rain fell that was more acid than vinegar.
5. In the 1920s, the IRS not only collected taxes but was the enforcer of the prohibition of alcohol.

Transitive/Intransitive Verbs
Identify each verb and decide if it's transitive or intransitive. If it's transitive, identify its object.
1. James composes lyrics but does not sing in tune.
2. Time flies at times.
3. She opened the door a crack and listened.
4, Shall we join the others or just stay here?
5. Before she wrote novels, she seldom read them.

Linking Verbs
Identify each verb (along with any helping verbs) as an action verb or linking verb.
1. In 1787, Lt. William Bligh became commander of the *Bounty,* a ship the British Royal Naval bought and fitted with canons. It would sail to Tahiti, collect breadfruit plants, and transport them to

the West Indies. They hoped breadfruit would grow there and be a cheap food source.

2. Weather conditions at Cape Horn made the *Bounty* change course and detour across the Indian Ocean. This cost an additional ten months.

3. When the *Bounty* finally arrived in Tahiti, the breadfruit were no longer in season. The crew lived onshore for five months as they waited for harvest time and enjoyed Tahiti. When the time arrived, they loaded 1,015 plants and stored them below deck. Many in the crew grew surly. They did not want to board ship and leave Tahiti.

4. Once underway, the crew became angry when they discovered how much space the breadfruit occupied. The overcrowded conditions were like a spark to tinder, and some 1,300 miles west of Tahiti, the crew staged a mutiny. They forced Bligh and 18 others into a small boat and abandoned them at sea.

5. Eventually Bligh and his men reached England, but not before they had sailed 43 days on a voyage that covered 600 miles. They navigated with sextant and a pocket watch.

6. The mutineers sailed back to Tahiti. Most were captured and sent to England for trial. But nine mutineers fled on the *Bounty* to Pitcairn Island and settled there, where they hoped they could elude the Royal Navy. Later, they burned the *Bounty*. They remained undetected. Eighteen years later, a Boston ship's captain discovered the one remaining mutineer on the island.

Principal Parts of Verbs

Complete the following sentences with the correct form of the verb in parentheses.

1. (*write*) Have you ____ your letter yet?
2 (*ring*) Has the bell ____? Yes, I ____ it.
3. (*go*) Have they ____ yet?
4. (*burst*) She has ____ the balloon.
5. (
swim) She ____ two miles, but she hasn't ____ as far
   as you have.
6. (*hang*) The convict was ____ yesterday.
7. (*come*) Has the mail ____ yet?
8. (*grow*) He has ____ three inches this year.
9. (*flee*) The refugees have ____ from the city.
10. (*blow*) the wind has ____ the tree down.
11. (*begin*) You ____ too late.
12. (*beat*) Which team was ____?
13. (*bring*) They ____ their dog with them.
14. (*ask*) I ____her to do it now.
15. (*break*) The window has been ____ twice.
16. (*fly*) The pilot has never ____ a jet plane before.
17. (*flow*) Water has ____ over the dam for years.
18. (*swing*) I ____ the children until they had ____
   long enough.
19. (*jump*) I have never ____ off a diving board.
20. (*talk*) Have you ____ about your vacation plans?

Person

In each sentence, identify the verb and decide whether it is first, second, or third person.

1. Do you agree with Karen?
2. I finished my term paper.
3. Today is a national holiday.
4. They are late again.
5. Did all of you finish the test?

Number

In each sentence, identify the verb and decide if it's singular or plural.

1. He never reads a newspaper.
2. We always meet on Tuesday.
3. My cousin works at the supermarket.
4. Rain freezes at these temperatures.
5. The band plays at the half-time show.

Tenses

Decide on the correct form of the verb in each sentence. If the verb form is incorrect, correct it. Some of the sentences are correct as they stand.

1. The veterinarian *examined* the horse.
2. He *has dove* off the cliff many times before.
3. We *done* our work early.
4. She *drawed* a good picture.
5. Have you *withdrawed* your money from the bank?
6. Have they *drunk* their coffee?
7. We have *ate* our lunch.
8. That hummingbird has *flew* from Mexico.
9. I have *swum* across the river many times.
10. They could not keep the dam from *busting*.
11. Would you mind if I *brang* my dog?
12. I *blowed* on my fingers to keep them warm.
13. The symphony concerts are *broadcast* on Sunday.
14. Much damage was done when the Mississippi *overflew* its banks.
15. Were the papers *throwed* away?
16. We had *hung* all the curtains by noon.
17. He has already *drank* the milk.
18. The water has *flown* over the sink.
19. I am afraid the water pipe has *bursted.*

20. She *ask* us several times, but we refused.
21. The monkey *swang* on a vine.
22. We *drug* the log to the campfire.
23. He thought his car had been *stoldt*.
24. The cashier *rung* up the wrong amount.
25. Has anyone *seen* Harvey?
26. I should have *brung* back your lawn mower.
27. I *throwed* the ball too far.
28. The passengers *fled* the burning ship.
29. You shouldn't have *et* those mushrooms.
30. Have you ever *growed* asparagus?

Active and Passive Voice
  Decide if each of the following sentences is active or passive.

1. The whole school participates in the fair.
2. An accident was prevented by her quick thinking.
3. The leading role was played brilliantly by Carson.
4. The movie was reviewed unfavorably by critics.
5. She recognized a celebrity in the crowd.
6. At first, her advice was ignored.
7. The host usually invites the guests.
8. Tourists from many countries visit the Alamo.
9. The rumors of a revolution were denied by the dictator.
10. The message was quickly delivered to the president

Mood: Indicative, Imperative, Subjunctive
  Identify whether the verb is in the indicative, imperative, or subjunctive mood.

1. Class, line up alphabetically, according to size.
2. If only I hadn't missed my flight.
3. Some say that a book is judged by its cover.

4. Don't forget to buy cheese.
5. This recipe calls for fresh basil.
6. I wish I were talented in art.
7. Please pass the mustard.
8. If I were you, I'd leave immediately.
9. That sentence expresses a condition contrary to fact.
10. If I were rich, I'd buy an Irish wolfhound.

Verbals

In the sentences below, verbals are in italics. Identify each as a gerund, past participle, or infinitive.

1. My favorite activity is *traveling*.
2. *Winning* the championship is their only goal.
3. *To go* or *to stay*, that is the question.
4. Use this puppy treat *to reward* Fang.
5. Can the *broken* plate be fixed?

CHAPTER 3
VERBS: ANSWERS

Action and Linking Verbs
1. is (*linking*)
2. banned (*action*); was (*linking*);
3. left (*action*); grew (*linking*)
4. fell (*action*); was (*linking*)
5. collected (*action*) was (*linking*)

Transitive/Intransitive Verbs
1. composes (*transitive: object*, lyrics); sing (*intransitive*)
2. flies (*intransitive*); say (*intransitive*)
3. opened (*transitive: object*, door); listened (*intransitive*)
4. shall join (*transitive: object*, others); stay (*intransitive*)
5. wrote (*transitive: object*, novels); read (*transitive: object*, them.)

Action Verbs and Linking Verbs
1. became (*linking*); bought (*action*); fitted (*action*); would sail (*action*); collect (*action*); transport (action); hoped (action); would grow (*action*); *be* (linking).
2. made (*action*); change (*action*); detour (*action*); was (*linking*); cost (*action*)
3. arrived (*action*); were (*linking*); lived (*action*); waited (*action*); enjoyed (*action*); arrived (*action*); loaded (*action*); stored (*action*); grew (*linking*); liked (*action*

4. became (*linking*); discovered (*action*); occupied (*action*); were (*linking*); staged (*action*): forced (*action*); abandoned (*action*).
5. reached (*action*); had sailed (*action*); covered (*action*); navigated (*action*).
6. sailed (*action*); were captured (*action*); sent (*action*); fled (*action*); settled (*action*); hoped (*action*); could elude (*action*); burned (*action*); remained (*linking*); discovered (*action*

Principal Parts of Verbs

1. written
2. rung; rang
3. gone
4. burst
5. swam; swum
6. hanged
7. come
8. grown
9. fled
10. blown
11. began
12. beaten
13. brought
14. asked
15. broken
16. flown
17. flowed
18. swung; swung
19. jumped
20. talked

Person

1. agree (2nd)
2. finished (1st)

3. is (3rd)
4. are (3rd)
5. finish (2nd)

Number
1. reads (singular)
2. meet (plural)
3. works (singular)
4. freezes (singular)
5. plays (singular)

Tenses
1. examined (correct)
2. has dived
3. did
4. drew
5. withdrawn
6. drunk
7. eaten
8. flown
9. swum
10. bursting
11. brought
12. blew
13. broadcast (correct)
14. overflowed
15. thrown
16. hung (correct)
17. drunk
18. flowed
19. burst
20. asked
21. swung
22. dragged
23. stolen

24. rang
25. seen (correct)
26. brought
27. threw
28. fled (correct)
29. eaten
30. grown

Active and Passive Voice
1. active
2. passive
3. passive
4. passive
5. active
6. passive
7. active
8. active
9. passive
10. passive

Mood: Indicative, Imperative, Subjunctive
1. imperative
2. subjunctive
3. indicative
4. imperative
5. indicative
6. subjunctive
7. imperative
8. subjunctive
9. indicative
10. subjunctive

Verbals
1. gerund
2. gerund

3. infinitive
4. infinitive
5. past participle

CHAPTER 4

ADJECTIVES

An adjective is a word that modifies (describes) a noun or pronoun or makes its meaning more exact.

FUNCTION OF ADJECTIVES

Grammar books like to say: "An adjective is a word that *modifies* a noun or pronoun." *Modify* comes from a Latin word meaning "to limit," in other words, "to make more exact."

An adjective answers one of these questions about a noun or pronoun:
1. Which?
2. What kind of?
3. How many?

See the table below for examples. Adjectives are in **bold** type.

WHICH?	WHAT KIND OF?	HOW MANY?
this book	**purple** bicycle	**seven** roses
last weekend	**plastic** jar	**an** hour
next Thursday	**complicated** problem	**few** people
second chapter	**large** boulder	**several** days

ARTICLES: *A, AN,* AND *THE*

The most commonly used adjectives are *a, an,* and *the.* In grammar, they are called **articles**. Articles are also called noun markers because they mark, or indicate, that a noun follows.

A and ***an*** answer the question *"how many?"* about a noun. Both *a* and *an* mean *one*: *a* pencil = one pencil; *an* umbrella = one umbrella. For ease of pronunciation, *a* is used before a noun that begins with a consonant. *An* is used before a noun that begins with a vowel sound.

The article ***the*** answers *"which?"* about a noun. "The" refers to a specific noun that was already mentioned. The reader will understand which noun is meant.

Examples:

> **The** *clock* struck one. (Which clock? The clock already mentioned.)

> **The** train arrived. (Which train? The train already mentioned.)

Indefinite Articles: *A, An*

A and *an* are called **indefinite articles** because they do not point to a definite person, place, or thing. Instead, they refer to one out of a general, indefinite, group. For example, if you say, "I want **a** dog," you aren't referring to one specific dog, but to any dog. It doesn't matter which one. If you ask, "Do you have **an** umbrella?" you are not asking about one specific umbrella but to any umbrella. It doesn't matter which one.

Here are the rules for using **a** and **an**:

1. Use **a** before a word that begins with a consonant sound (e.g.," a salad").
2. Use **an** before a word that begins with a vowel sound (e.g., "**an** egg"). This is done for ease in pronunciation.

Note that in determining whether to use *a* or *an* before a word beginning with a consonant, it is the *sound* of the consonant letter that is important. Some words begin with a consonant letter that is silent. For example, the word *hour* begins with a consonant letter, *h,* but the *h* in *hour* is silent. Since *hour* does not begin with a consonant *sound, an* is correct. We say *an hour,* not *a hour* (which would be difficult to pronounce).

The consonant sound of *h* is the sound of *h* in the word *heart.* Since *heart* begins with a consonant *sound, a* is correct. We say *a heart,* not *an heart.*

Definite Article: *The*

The article **the** points to a definite person, place or thing — a specific noun. Appropriately, the term for "the" is: **definite article**. If you say, "Did you see **the** movie?" you are talking about a definite movie, not just any movie. You can be sure your listener knows exactly which movie you mean because you've already been talking about that movie. Here are some more examples:

Do you want to go to **the** *party*?

Yes, I mailed **the** *letter* this morning.

Read **the** *instructions.*

USING ADJECTIVES IN SENTENCES

Before a Noun

An adjective comes before the noun it modifies. This is the normal word order. (In the examples below, adjectives are in bold type, and the nouns they modify are in italics.):

1. The **quick brown** *fox* jumped over the **lazy, indifferent** *dog*.
2. The **agile, swift young** *fox* jumped over the **fat, lazy** *dog*.
3. We left **magnificent, beloved** *Rome* in **clear sunset** *light*.
4. A herd of **some thirty huge grey** *oxen* were feeding on **one** *hill*.

Separating Adjectives With Commas

Notice in the examples above that a noun may have more than one adjective describing it. Some adjectives are separated by commas; some are not. How can you tell when to separate adjectives with commas? Here are two tricks: (1) If you can say "and" between the two adjectives and it makes sense, use a comma. If not, don't use a comma. (2) If you can reverse the order of two adjectives, put a comma between them (e.g., young, agile fox *reversed to* agile, young fox). If you can't switch the adjectives, don't use a comma.

Note: If English is not your native language, you may have to focus on the placement of adjectives *before* a noun. This is the customary position in Germanic languages. Many languages, however, place adjectives *after* nouns. Some of these languages are: French, Italian, Spanish, Portuguese, Hebrew, Romanian, Arabic, Persian Vietnamese, and Swahili.

Order of Adjectives

When a noun has more than one adjective modifying it there is a certain order in which these adjectives appear. Native speakers of English usually have no problem with this because a sentence will "sound right" if its adjectives are in order. If English is your second language, however, the order of adjectives can be a problem because the order is different in other languages. Here is the order of adjectives in English:

1. **Number** (a specific number or an *indefinite* quantity like "some")
2. **Quality, value, or opinion of quality** (good, bad, exceptional, significant, etc.)
3. **Size** (big, small, etc.)
4. **Temperature** (hot, cold, etc.)
5. **Age** (old, new, young, etc.)
6. **Shape** (round, square, etc.)
7. **Color** (blue, red, yellow, etc.)
8. **Origin** (Where did it come from? E.g., India.)
9. **Material** (cotton, wood, cloth, stone, etc.)

An adjective usually comes immediately *before* the noun or pronoun it modifies. (See the example sentences below. Nouns are underlined.)

1. A *huge* boulder blocked the road.
2. She wrote a *long, complicated* report.
3. He has *dark, brooding* eyes.
4. *Three small, baby* turtles crawled down the *muddy* bank.

Predicate Adjectives

As mentioned above, an adjective usually comes *before* the noun or pronoun it modifies. It can come after the word it modifies, however, *if* that word is followed by a *linking verb* (e.g., *is, was*). In that case, the adjective comes *after* the linking verb. For example, if we change the first sentence in the above list to, "The boulder **was** *huge*," *huge* is still an adjective modifying the noun *boulder*, but it is separated from the noun by the linking verb *was*. The pattern is: noun – linking verb – adjective

When an adjective *follows* a linking verb it is called a **predicate adjective**. Why? Because it comes in the *predicate* part of the sentence. The predicate of a sentence begins with the verb. The *predicate* is the part of the sentence that tells what the subject *is* or *does*. (In other words, the predicate is everything that is not the subject.)

In the sentence, "The boulder was huge," *huge* is a predicate adjective that describes *boulder*. The verb, *was*, is a linking verb.

Forms of the linking verb *be* are those most likely to be followed by a predicate adjective. Other linking verbs, however, may also be followed by a predicate adjective.

REMINDER. Other linking verbs include verbs of the senses (*see, hear, smell, taste, feel*) and a few others, such as *appear, become, grow, seem, stand, ring,* and *prove.*

Note that predicate adjectives only follow linking verbs, not action verbs. Thus, in the sentence, "The rose *smells* sweet," the verb *smells* is a linking verb, and *sweet* is a predicate adjective. But in the sentence, "He *smells* a sweet rose," the verb *smells* is an action verb and cannot be followed by a predicate adjective. (*Sweet* is an adjective and comes before the noun it modifies, *rose*.)

More examples. In the sentences below, the verbs are linking verbs (not action verbs). They are followed by predicate adjectives. Notice that in each sentence you can substitute a form of the verb *be* for the verb. This indicates that the verb is a linking verb.

1. Sheldon looks *tired*. (*is* tired)
2. The music sounds *faint*. (*is* faint)
3. The thorns *feel* sharp. (*are* sharp)
4. I feel *calm*. (*am* calm)
5. The ground grew *firm*. (*was* firm)
6. She appeared *friendly*. (*was* friendly)
7. He proved *untrustworthy*. (*was* untrustworthy)
8. The men stood *silent*. (*were* silent)

SUMMARY: The two positions of the adjective in a sentence are: (1) preceding a noun or pronoun; (2) following a linking verb.

PROPER ADJECTIVES AND DEMONSTRATIVE ADJECTIVES

Proper Adjectives

In the chapter on nouns, you learned:
1. A proper noun names a specific person, place, thing, or idea.
2. A proper noun begins with a capital letter.

Proper adjectives are adjectives formed from proper nouns. Like proper nouns, proper adjectives are capitalized. This includes adjectives used in brand names.

Examples of proper adjectives are listed below. The adjectives are in italics:

<u>*Examples*</u>:

Mexican food
French language
Harvard graduate
Achilles tendon
Roman architecture
Shakespearean sonnets
Jeffersonian philosophy
Scandinavian winter
June day
Ford truck
Victorian poetry
Idaho potato
Texas toast
Jamaican music
Stephen King novel
Monet painting
Caribbean port
Greek myth
Egyptian hieroglyphs
Labrador retriever

Prefixes attached to proper adjectives are *not* capitalized unless the prefixes are formed from a proper noun (e.g., *Afro-American*).

<u>*Examples:*</u>

pro-Communist
pre-Raphaelite

Afro-Caribbean
Pan-American
anti-West

In a hyphenated word, *only* the proper adjective is capitalized.

<u>*Examples:*</u><u>*Portuguese-speaking Brazilians*</u>

English-speaking guide

Demonstrative Adjectives

In the chapter on pronouns, you read about demonstrative pronouns: *this, that, these,* and *those.* Those same words become **demonstrative adjectives** when they immediately precede a noun.

<u>*Examples*</u>:

This is my bracelet. (demonstrative pronoun)

This bracelet is mine. (demonstrative adjective modifying *bracelet*)

Demonstrative adjectives point out the nouns they describe. Like the demonstrative pronouns *this* and *these,* the demonstrative adjectives *this* and *these* point out something nearby. The demonstrative adjectives *that* and *those* point out something farther away. Demonstrative adjectives answer the question "Which?" about a noun: e.g., "Which dog?" "*This* dog."

USING ADJECTIVES TO MAKE COMPARISONS

Adjectives can be used to show comparisons. They do this by adding the endings *-er* or *-est.* The simple form of an adjective is called the *positive* form. It is used for basic description, as in the sentence, "Kelly is *tall.*" If we want to compare the

height of Angela with the height of Kelly, we use
another form of the adjective – the *comparative*
form – and we say, "Angela is *taller* than Kelly." If
we want to compare Macy's height with that of
Angela and Kelly, we use still another form of the
adjective – the *superlative* form —and we say, "Macy
is the *tallest* of all."

1. Kelly is *tall. (Positive)*

2. Angela is *taller* than Kelly. *(Comparative)*

3. Macy is the *tallest* of all. *(Superlative)*

Degrees of Comparison

The adjective forms used for comparisons are
called **degrees.** Thus, the three degrees of
comparison are: (1) *positive degree,* (2) *comparative
degree,* (3) *superlative degree.*

SUMMARY: The *positive degree* of an adjective is
simply descriptive. The *comparative degree*
compares two things only. The *superlative
degree* compares three or more things.

Forming the Comparative and Superlative

The usual way to form the comparative and
superlative of short adjectives is to add *-er* to the
positive to form the comparative, and add *-est* to the
positive to form the superlative:

Positive	Comparative	Superlative
young	younger	youngest
large	larger	largest
cold	colder	coldest
sharp	sharper	sharpest

Although short adjectives add *-er* and *-est* to form comparisons, many adjectives of two or more syllables would sound lengthy and awkward if *-er* and *-est* were added. It would sound awkward, for example, to say "intelligenter" and "intelligentest." Thus, we compare the adjective *intelligent* by using the forms *more intelligent* and *most intelligent*.

Positive	Comparative	Superlative
beautiful	more beautiful	most beautiful
careful	more careful	most careful
active	more active	most active
ferocious	more ferocious	most ferocious

Irregular Comparison Forms

A few adjectives change their forms completely for comparisons. The table below shows some of these.

Positive	Comparative	Superlative
good	better	best
bad	worse	worst
little	less	least
much	more	most
far	farther	farthest

Error: Double Comparisons

Don't make double comparisons. That is, don't use both *-er* and *more* or *-est* and *most* to form comparatives or superlatives.

Incorrect:

Which is the *more bigger* dessert?
Which is the *most sweetest* dessert?

Incomplete Comparisons

Is it correct to say, "The whale is larger than any animal in the world"? At first thought, it seems correct. However, the whale is an animal in the world. A whale can't be larger that itself, can it? The comparison is incomplete without adding the word *other* to make the sentence read: "The whale is larger than any other animal in the world." In the same way, the comparison "Madison was shorter than any of our presidents" is incomplete because Madison was a president. The sentence should be changed to read, "Madison was shorter than any other of our presidents" or "any of our other presidents."

Adjectives that Cannot Be Compared

There are some adjectives that in their strict sense cannot be compared. These include: *empty, perfect, exact, correct, immortal, eternal, omnipotent, infinite, dead,* and *complete.* For example, is something is perfect, it can't be made *more perfect.* Thus, do not use "more" or "most" with adjectives that can't be compared.

CHAPTER 4

ADJECTIVES: CHECK-UP

(Scroll down for answers.)

Articles

Identify the articles in the following sentences.
1. The clock on the landing is an antique.
2. A penny saved is a penny earned, the saying goes.
3. Is eating an apple a day a healthy eating habit?
4. The recipe calls for a cup of flour, an ounce of sugar, and a pinch of salt.
5. An alligator, a dragon, and an ostrich walked into the restaurant.

Separating Adjectives with Commas

Decide where to place commas between adjectives in the sentences below.

1. We had to travel on narrow dark treacherous unpaved country roads.
2. A tall thin brown-haired blue-eyed child sat on a sawed-off old oak log.
3. We anticipated a long tedious five-hour business meeting.
4. I longed to own a soft pale blue long-sleeve expensive cashmere sweater.
5. Two mouth-watering buckwheat pancakes were served with organic Vermont maple syrup.

Order of Adjectives

Put the following list of adjectives in the order they should appear in a sentence.

1. American
2. emerald-green
3. shoddy
4. tiny
5. seventeen
6. ancient
7. marble
8. oval
9. frigid

Predicate Adjectives

Identify the predicate adjectives in the following sentences.

1. Although the lecture was interesting, it grew lengthy.
2. Ordinarily, Janet is agreeable, but today she seems grumpy.
3. The stone's surface felt cold and rough.
4. It will become warm and sunny after 2:00.
5. Something in the shed smells rancid.

Proper and Demonstrative Adjectives

Identify the proper adjectives and demonstrative adjectives in the following sentences.
1. Have you read that Stephen King novel?
2. I am deciding between this Siberian husky and that Boston terrier.
3. On that lovely June day, I sat under a tree, reading this book of Victorian poetry
4. That old Ford truck pulled into that Mexican restaurant an hour ago.
5. The key to translating Egyptian hieroglyphics came from a stone that is now in this British museum.

Using Adjectives to Make Comparisons

Give the comparative and superlative forms of the adjectives in the list below.

1. little (meaning "small amount")
2. much
3. near
4. bad
5. hard
6. miserable
7. popular
8. soft
9. skillful
10. sudden

Correct the following sentences.

1. Is electricity the most usefullest of today's conveniences?
2. They can manage the children much easier than I can.
3. Which of these two coats do you think is the most expensive?
4. She achieved more than any mayor they had ever known.
5. Do you think she likes Mark or me best?

6. Of all the fish in the tank, the bettas were prettier.

CHAPTER 4

ADJECTIVES: ANSWERS

Articles
1. The, the, an
2. A, a, the
3. an, a, a
4. The, a, an, a
5. An, a, an, the

Separating Adjectives with Commas
1. We had to travel on narrow, dark, treacherous, unpaved country roads.
2. A tall, thin, brown-haired, blue-eyed child sat on a sawed-off, old oak log.
3. We anticipated a long, tedious five-hour business meeting.
4. I longed to own a soft, pale blue, long-sleeve, expensive cashmere sweater.
5. Two mouth-watering buckwheat pancakes were served with organic Vermont maple syrup.

Order of Adjectives
1. seventeen
2. shoddy
3. tiny
4. frigid
5. ancient
6. oval
7. emerald-green
8. American
9. marble

Predicate Adjectives
1. interesting, lengthy

2. agreeable, grumpy
3. cold, rough
4. warm, sunny
5. rancid

Proper and Demonstrative Adjectives
1. that, Stephen King
2. this, Siberian, that, Boston
3. that, June, this, Victorian
4. That, Ford, that, Mexican
5. Egyptian, this

Using Adjectives to Make Comparisons
1. less, least
2. more, most
3. nearer, nearest
4. worse, worst
5. harder, hardest
6. more miserable, most miserable
7. more popular, most popular
8. softer, softest
9. more skillful, most skillful
10. more sudden, most sudden

1. Is electricity the most useful of today's conveniences?
2. They can manage the children more easily than I can.
3. Which of these two coats do you think is the more expensive?
4. She achieved more than any other mayor they had ever known.
5. Do you think she likes Mark or me better?
6. Of all the fish in the tank, the bettas were prettiest.

CHAPTER FIVE

ADVERBS

An adverb is a word used to modify (describe) a verb, adjective, or another adverb.

USING ADVERBS IN SENTENCES

Adverbs and adjectives are similar. They are both words used to modify (describe) other words. Adjectives modify nouns and pronouns. Adverbs modify verbs, adjectives, and other adverbs.

In the examples below, adverbs are in **bold** type, and the words they modify are in *italics*.

Adverb describing a verb:

The line *moved* **forward**.
The dog *stood* **quietly** by her side.

Adverb describing an *adjective*:

The blade was **very** *sharp*.
The house was **strangely** *silent*.

Adverb describing another adverb:

James is **almost** *always* late.
We had met **rather** *recently*.

An adverb usually answers one of these questions about the word it describes: ***How? When? Where? To what extent?***

The dog stood **quietly**. (Stood how? *quietly*)
We had met **recently**. (Met when? *recently*)
They moved **forward** (Moved where? *forward*)
Daniel **scarcely** slept. (Slept to what extent? *scarcely*)

Position in Sentence

An adverb that modifies a verb can come almost anywhere in a sentence, but an adverb that modifies an adjective or another adverb usually comes directly before the word it modifies.

<u>*Examples:*</u>

> 1. The blade was **very** sharp. (Very modifies the adjective *sharp*.)
> 2. We had met **rather** recently. (*Rather* modifies the adverb *recently*.)

ADVERB FORMS

Most adverbs end in *-ly*. Adverbs are often formed by adding *-ly* to an adjective (e.g., *quick/quickly* and *beautiful/beautifully*).

Some commonly used adverbs, however, do not end in *-ly*, including the two most frequently used adverbs, *too* and *very*. See the following list of other common adverbs that do not end in *-ly*.

COMMONLY USED ADVERBS

<u>*Examples:*</u>

afterward
almost
already
back
even
far
fast

hard
here
high
how
late
long
low
more
never
next
not
now
often
quick
rather
right
slow
so
somewhat
wide
yesterday

ADJECTIVE OR ADVERB?

The words in the list below may be either adjectives or adverbs. How can you tell the difference? You need to determine how they are used. If the word modifies a noun or pronoun, it is an adjective. If it modifies a verb, adjective, or adverb, it is an adverb. If you familiarize yourself with the words in the list you will minimize your confusion about them.

1. best
2. better
3. bright
4. cheap
5. early

6. fair
7. far
8. fast
9. just
10. long

11. loud
12. sharp
13. short
14. slow

15. soft

COMPARISONS WITH ADVERBS

Adverbs are used to show comparisons, just as adjectives are. Most adverbs use *more* and *most* to form the comparative and superlative degrees, although a few use the *-er* and *-est* forms. Like adjectives, some adverbs are irregular and change their form entirely to show comparisons. The table below illustrates how to form the comparative and superlative forms of adverbs.

Adverb	Comparative	Superlative
Add – *er* and – *est* to most one-syllable adverbs.		
wide	wider	widest
soon	sooner	soonest
fast	faster	fastest
Use *more* and *most* before most adverbs of two or more syllables.		
quietly	more quietly	most quietly
easily	more easily	most easily
clearly	more clearly	most clearly

IRREGULAR COMPARATIVES
AND SUPERLATIVES

There are a few common adverbs that have irregular comparative and superlative forms that you just have to learn. They are listed below

Adverb	Comparative	Superlative
badly	worse	worst
well	better	best
little	less	least
much	more	most
far	farther	farthest
	(or *further*)	(or *furthest*)

SUMMARY: An adverb is a word that modifies a verb, an adjective, or another adverb.

Many adverbs have a comparative and a superlative form used for comparisons.

An adverb answers one of these questions about the word it modifies: *How? Where? When?* and *To what extent?*

CHAPTER 5

ADVERBS: CHECK-UP

(Scroll down for answers.)

Adverb Forms

Identify the adverbs in the following sentences.
1. They went quickly to their house.
2. She felt awkwardly about her remark.
3. A very large dog stood at the gate.
4. The bell rang unusually loud.
5. I looked up slowly from my work.
6. Music sounded faintly over the water.
7. The surgeon calmly felt the injured wrist.
8. He amicably appeared in response to the applause.
9. The fungus grows firmly on the tree.
10. He proved his statements willingly.
11. We stood quietly at the door.
12. You spoke the best of all.
13. They ran fast to catch the train.
14. They worked hard on the assignment.
15. The puppy behaved badly.

Adverb or Adjective?

Determine which words are adjectives and which are adverbs in the following sentences. (Don't include articles as adjectives.)

1. He seemed very happy when I last saw him.
2. Napoleon Hill's *Think and Grow Rich* is an extremely interesting book.
3. Mark's genial, booming laugh sounded good to me.
4. I am tired of your empty promises.

5. It grew rather dark, and the waves became
   increasingly rough.

    Decide whether the italicized word is an adjective or adverb, and decide what it modifies.

1. We rose *early* that morning.
2. I like dancing *better* than card games.
3. Elizabeth and Michelle felt *sick*.
4. He was *quick* to learn the game.
5. She saw the dog in the road, and stopped *short*.
6. "Swing *Low*, Sweet Chariot" is a famous spiritual.
7. We had an *early* breakfast and caught the next
   bus.
8. Colonel Mustard was known for his ability to
   shoot *straight*.
9. The weather is *rather* warm for February.
10. The hour is *late*, and we must go now.

Comparisons with Adverbs

    Give the comparative and superlative forms of the adverbs below.

1. hard
2. nearly
3. high
4. badly
5. fast
6. well
7. much
8. far
9. quietly
10. easily

CHAPTER 5
ADVERBS: ANSWERS

Adverb Forms
1. quickly
2. awkwardly
3. very
4. unusually
5. slowly
6. faintly
7. calmly
8. amicably
9. firmly
10. willingly
11. quietly
12. best
13. fast
14. hard
15. badly

Adverb or Adjective?
1. very (adverb); happy (adjective)
2. extremely (adverb); interesting (adjective)
3. genial, booming, good (adjectives)
4. tired, empty (adjectives)
5. rather, increasingly (adverbs); dark, rough (adjectives)

1. *Early* is an adverb modifying the verb *rose*.
2. *Better* is an adverb modifying the verb *like*.
3. *Sick* is an adjective modifying the nouns *Elizabeth* and *Michelle*.
4. -*Quick* is an adjective modifying the pronoun *he.*

5. *Short* is an adverb modifying the verb *stopped.*
6. *Low* is an adverb modifying the verb *swing.*
7. *Early* is an adjective modifying the noun breakfast; *next* is an adjective modifying the noun *bus.*
8. *Straight* is an adverb modifying the verb *shoot.*
9. *Rather* is an adverb modifying the adjective *warm.*
10. *Late* is an adjective modifying the noun *hour; now* is an adverb modifying the verb *go.*

Comparisons with Adverbs
1. harder, hardest
2. more nearly, most nearly
3. higher, highest
4. worse, worst
5. faster, fastest
6. better, best
7. more , most
8. farther, farthest
9. more quietly, most quietly
10. more easily, most easily

PREPOSITIONS

A preposition is a word that shows a relationship between a noun or pronoun and another word or element in the sentence.

Prepositions are small words, but they can make a big difference in meaning. In the following sentences, the prepositions are in bold type. Notice how they change the meaning of each sentence:

1. Water rushes **under** the bridge.
2. Water rushes **over** the bridge.

3. I like to take a run **before** breakfast.
4. I like to take a run **after** breakfast.

5. The train **to** Washington is late.
6. The train **from** Washington is late.

FUNCTION OF PREPOSITIONS

Prepositions link two words and show their relationship – usually their relationship in space, time, or direction. In sentences 1 and 2 above, the prepositions *under* and *over* link the nouns *water* and *bridge* and show their relationship in space. Can you picture the differences in meaning between sentences 1 and 2 – the difference in space between *under* and *over*?

In sentences 3 and 4 the prepositions *before* and *after* link the nouns *run* and *breakfast. Run* is related to breakfast by time, the time before or after the event of breakfast. In sentences 5 and 6 the prepositions *to* and *from* link the nouns *train* and *Washington* by direction — to and from.

The illustration below shows common prepositions that indicate relationships in space, such as *above, below, inside, outside.* Prepositions such as *before, after, during* show relationships in time; and prepositions such as *toward, across, around* show direction.

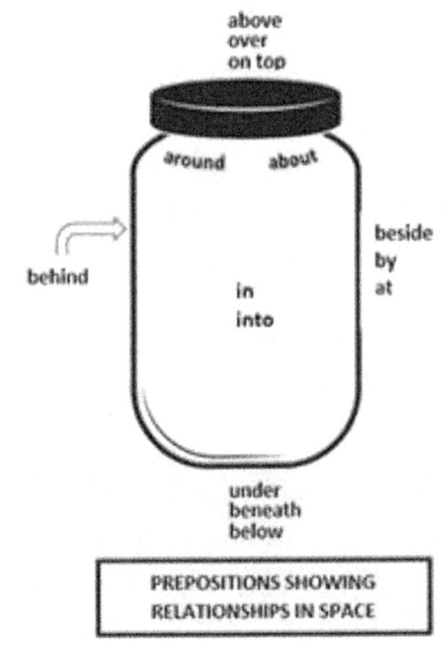

COMMON PREPOSITIONS

The following table lists commonly used prepositions. Read them over and think about which show a relationship of space, time, or direction.

PREPOSITIONS		
aboard	but (meaning "except")	past
about	by	since
above	concerning	through
across	despite	throughout
after	down	till
against	during	to
along	except	toward
among	for	under
around	from	underneath
at	inside	until
before	into	up
behind	like	upon
below	near	with
beneath	of	within
beside	off	without
besides	on	
between	out	
beyond	over	

The prepositions in the chart are simple, one-word prepositions. But some prepositions are made up of more than one word:

Examples:

> according to
> because of
> by way of
> due to
> in front of
> in regard to
> in response to

in spite of
instead of
on account of
on top of
out of

OBJECT OF THE PREPOSITION

The *pre* in *preposition* is a prefix meaning "before." A preposition is positioned, or placed, *before* a noun. A preposition is *always* followed by a noun or pronoun. That noun or pronoun is called the *object of the preposition.* For example, in the sentence "The book is on the table," the word *table* (the noun after the proposition *on*) is the object of the preposition.In the example below, the preposition *to* has three objects: *Mike, Joyce, me.*

Example:
James sent an invitation **to** *Mike, Joyce,* and *me.*

Object of Preposition vs. Object of Verb

In the chapter on verbs, you learned that *all transitive verbs take objects.* What is the difference between the object of a verb and the object of a preposition?

Remember that the object of a transitive verb is the receiver of the verb's action. For example, in the sentence, "She shot the arrow at the target," *arrow* is the object of the verb *shot.* (*Arrow* is the receiver of the action *shot.*)

Target is the object of the preposition *at. At the target* indicates the *direction* of the shot.

Look for the objects of the prepositions in the ten sentences below. The prepositions are italicized. In each sentence, the preposition is before the noun that is its object.

1. Put the dishes *in* the sink.
2. Lay the rug *on* the floor.
3. Check your receipt *from* the store.
4. The dog ran *across* the lawn.
5. I found this ring *among* the bushes.
6, The ball soared *over* the wall.
7. We inched our way *through* the undergrowth.
8. The key was hidden *under* a rock.
9. Drive *around* the block.
10. She stood *in front of* the restaurant.

Notice that in the last sentence, *in front of* is considered as a preposition.

PREPOSITIONAL PHRASE

A preposition, its object, and any words that describe the object make up *a prepositional phrase*. A prepositional phrase can be as short as two or three words: *to me . . . over the sea.* But it can be much longer. It all depends on the number of words that describe the object of the preposition. In the examples below, the prepositions are italicized.

Examples of Prepositional Phrases:

under the spreading chestnut tree
in the nick of time
with the mysterious talkative stranger
on top of Old Smoky
out of Africa
according to Hoyle

Adjective and Adverb Phrases

A prepositional phrase may act as an **adjective**, describing as a noun or pronoun. Or, it may act as an **adverb**, describing a verb, adjective or other adverb.

Adjective Phrases

Here are some examples of prepositional phrases used as *adjectives*. Notice that, like other adjectives, the phrase answers the question *Which? What kind of?* or *How many?* about a noun.

1. The box *with the pepperoni pizza* (Which box?)
2. Houses *on the waterfront* (What kind of houses?)
3. Dinner *for eight* (Dinner for how *many?*)

Notice that adjective phrases *follow* the noun or pronoun they modify. (This is different from simple adjectives, which usually come before the noun or pronoun they modify.)

Adverb Phrases

A prepositional phrase used as an *adverb* describes a verb, adjective, or other adverb and answers the question *How? Where? Why?* or *To what extent?* Here are some examples of prepositional phrases used as adverbs:

1. We descended *with great difficulty.* (Descended *how*?)
2. Something lies *beneath the surface.* (Lies *where?*)
3. Will it arrive *before his birthday?* (Arrive *when?*)
4. She succeeded *beyond her dreams.* (Succeeded *to what extent?*)

Adverb phrases may be located almost anywhere in a sentence. They can be separated from the word they modify.

Practicing Correct Phrases

Some prepositional phrases we commonly hear are used incorrectly. These are often phrases that have a pronoun (or pronouns) as their object. (Remember, some pronouns have a different form when they are used as objects.)

When we hear an incorrect phrase repeatedly, it sounds right to us. The only way to substitute it with the correct phrase is to repeat the correct phrase until it "sounds right" to our ears. All of the phrases below are correct. Read them aloud. If any phrase sounds wrong to you, repeat it until it "sounds right."

1. between you and me
2. between him and her
3. between them and us
4. to him and us
5. to her and me
6. from him and her
7. except you and us
8. for them and her
9. for you and him
10. with her and me
11, with him and them
12. with them and us

13, about you and me
14. beside them and me
15. like him and me.

CHAPTER 6
PREPOSITIONS: CHECK-UP

(Scroll down for answers.)

Common Prepositions

Identify the prepositions in the following sentences. (Consider phrases such as *on top of* as a single preposition).

1. Have you read *To the Lighthouse* by Virginia Woolf?
2. It is written from an unusual perspective.
3. It has readers peer into the characters' stream of consciousness and sift through their thoughts.
4. In the story, the Ramsey family and friends gather at their summer house on the Hebrides Islands off the coast of Scotland.
5. In regard to time in the novel, it is two days with ten years between them.

Identify the prepositions in this excerpt from Lincoln's "Gettysburg Address."

It is rather for us to be here dedicated to the great task remaining before us – that from these honored dead we take increased devotion to that cause for which they gave the last full measure of devotion; that we here highly resolve that these dead shall not have died in vain; that this nation under God shall have a new birth of freedom; and that government of the people, by the people, and for the people, shall not perish from the earth.

Object of the Preposition

Identify the preposition and object of the preposition in the following sentences.

1. Put the casserole in the oven.
2. The hummingbird landed on my finger.
3. Don't run from a bear.
4. I ran across the bridge.
5. What is moving among the trees?
6. The bear went over the mountain.
7. Sludging through mud was unpleasant.
8. Don't peek under the rug.
9. His store is just around the bend.
10. A truck was parked in front of the house.

Prepositional Phrases
　　Identify the prepositional phrases in each sentence and decide whether each is used as an adjective or adverb.

1. A cup of coffee sat on the counter.
2. During the last week of vacation, we will relax at the beach.
3. Let's leave at once to get the best seats for the show.
4. In English class, we are analyzing the plot of the book.
5. He ran through the woods and dashed into the cabin.
6. The man with one black shoe went behind the gym.
7. That shape under the bridge is moving like a turtle.
8. In the summer, I practice yoga on the beach.
9. The dog in the kennel behind the house barks with ferocity.
10. The resort in Maryville advertised at great expense for tourists.

CHAPTER 6
PREPOSITIONS: ANSWERS

Common Prepositions
1. to, by
2. from
3. into, of, through
4. in, at, on, off
5. in regard to, with, between

The prepositions in the excerpt are:
for (us), to (the great), before (us), from (these honored dead), to (that cause), for (which), of (devotion), in (vain), under (God), of (freedom), of (the people), by (the people), for (the people), from (the earth)

Object of the Preposition
1. in (preposition); oven (object)
2. on (preposition); finger (object)
3. from (preposition); bear (object)
4. across (preposition); bridge (object)
5. among (preposition); trees (object)
6. over (preposition); mountain (object)
7. through (preposition); mud (object)
8. under (preposition); rug (object)
9. around (preposition); bend (object)
10. in front of (preposition); house (object)

Prepositional Phrases
1. of coffee (adjective); on the counter (adverb)
2. of vacation (adjective); at the beach (adverb)
3. at once (adverb); for the show (adjective)
4. in English class (adverb); of the book (adjective)

5. through the woods (adverb); into the cabin
   (adverb)
6. with one black shoe (adjective); behind the gym
   (adverb)
7. under the bridge (adjective); like a turtle (adverb)
8. in the summer (adverb); on the beach (adverb)
9. in the kennel (adjective); behind the house
   (adjective); with ferocity (adverb)
10. in Maryville (adjective); at great expense
   (adverb); for tourists (adverb)

CHAPTER SEVEN
CONJUNCTIONS

The word *conjunction* comes from the Latin prefix *con-* meaning "with" or "together" and the verb *jungo,* meaning "join." Thus, a conjunction is used to join words or groups of words. Prepositions also join words together. But unlike a preposition, a conjunction never takes an object, and it shows a less definite relationship between the words it joins.

Knowing how to use conjunctions correctly will be invaluable in learning how to create effective sentences.

KINDS OF CONJUNCTIONS

There are three kinds of conjunctions:

    1. coordinating conjunctions

    2. correlative conjunctions

    3. subordinate conjunctions.

COORDINATING CONJUNCTIONS

The word *coordinating* means "equal in rank," and *coordinating conjunctions*, appropriately, join words or groups of words that are equal in some way.

The most common coordinating conjunctions are **and**, **or**, and **but**. Notice in the examples below that those coordinating conjunctions join words that are grammatically equal

<u>*Examples*</u>:
> ham *and* eggs (*and* joins two nouns)
> large *or* small (*or* joins two adjectives)
> do not run *but* walk (*but* joins two verbs)

Coordinating conjunctions are the most common kind of conjunctions. There are seven of them. You can remember them with the acronym FANBOYS: **for, and, nor, but, or, yet, so.**

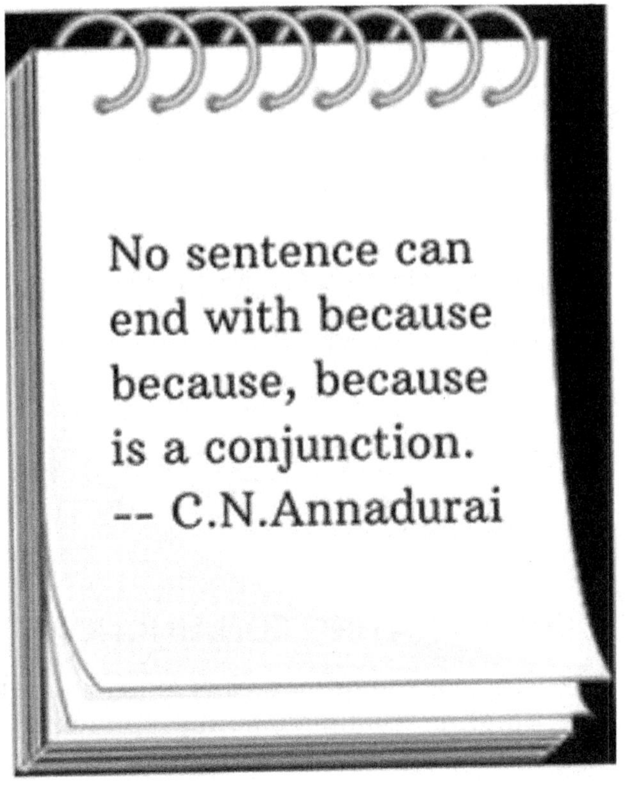

NOTE: The conjunction *for* can also be a preposition. How can you tell the difference? When *for* is a preposition it is followed by a noun or pronoun that is its object (e.g., "gift *for*

Juan"). When *for* is a conjunction it joins words or groups of words (e.g., "I am nervous, *for* it is growing dark.").

CORRELATIVE CONJUNCTIONS

Some conjunctions work in pairs. These pairs are called *correlative conjunctions*. *Correlative* means "corresponding, or complementing, each other"; "matching." The most common pairs of correlative conjunctions are shown in the table below.

Correlative Conjunctions
neither ... nor
not only ... but also
whether ... or
both... and
not ... but
as ... as
such ... that
as many ... as
scarcely ... when
no sooner ... than
rather ... than

Pairs of correlative conjunctions work together to connect either words or groups of words. The sentence parts they connect are usually equal. In the sentences that follow, correlative conjunctions are in bold type and the sentence parts they connect are in italics.

1. Angela is **not only** *daring* **but also** *clever.*
2. We will stay **either** *in Cairo* **or** *in Luxor.*
3. We'll stay at **both** *Cairo* **and** *Luxor.*
4. I don't know **whether** *Cairo* **or** *Luxor* is our first stop.
5. I have been to **neither** the Pyramids **nor** the Valley of the Kings.
6. We're in the mood **not** *for rest* **but** *for adventure*
7. Sunbathing isn't **as** *intriguing* **as** *sightseeing.*
8. *We had* **scarcely** *reached* our tent **when** *we received* visitors.

The important thing to remember is that correlative conjunctions join sentence parts that are parallel, or equal.

SUBORDINATING CONJUNCTIONS

Subordinating conjunctions are words that join independent clauses with subordinate clauses. What does that mean? Some definitions are in order.

Clauses: Independent and Subordinate

Clause: A clause is a group of words that has a subject and a verb.

Independent Clause: An independent clause can stand alone as a simple sentence. The example sentence below contains two independent clauses joined by a comma and the coordinating conjunction *and.* The independent clauses are in italics.

<u>*Example:*</u>

> *We went to the theater early,* and *we got really good seats.*

The two independent clauses could be written with a semicolon between them:

> *We went to the theater early; we got really good seats.*

They could also be written as two separate sentences.

> *We went to the theater early. We got really good seats.*

Subordinate Clause: *Subordinate* means "of lesser rank or importance."

Subordinate clauses cannot stand alone as sentences. Since they cannot stand alone as independent sentences, some grammar books call them *dependent clauses.* Subordinate clauses are subordinate to (of lesser importance than) independent clauses.

Subordinate clauses function in a sentence as adjectives, adverbs, or nouns – that is, as an adjective clause, an adverb clause, or a noun clause.

Subordinating Conjunctions

Subordinating conjunctions are used to connect subordinate clauses with independent clauses. In the examples below, the subordinate clauses are in italics. Each subordinate clause begins with a subordinating conjunction of one or more words. If you say each subordinate clause aloud, you will see that each needs an independent clause to make its meaning clear.

1. I turned off the lights *before I left*

2. We were late *because traffic was heavy.*

3. We'll go to the game tomorrow *unless it rains.*

4. A reception will be held *after the wedding.*

5. *As she went to the door,* she tripped.

6. He began to yawn *because the speech was so boring.*

7. I followed his advice *although I felt uneasy.*

8. We'll have a picnic *even if it rains.*

9. Please let me know *if you find my wallet.*

10. Read the directions *in order to avoid problems.*

11. I'll expect you tomorrow *unless I hear from you.*

12. Continue working *until the bell rings.*

13. *Whenever I hear a siren,* I cringe.

14. Let's follow the road *wherever it goes.*

15. The music blared on *while I tried to sleep.*

Common subordinating conjunctions are shown in the table below. Notice that some conjunctions are more than one word.

Subordinating Conjunctions		
after	even though	than
although	if	then
as	in order to	that
as if	once	though
as though	provided that	unless
because	rather than	until
before	since	when
even if	so that	whenever

CHAPTER 7

CONJUNCTIONS: CHECK-UP

(Scroll down for answers.)

Coordinating Conjunctions

Identify the coordinating conjunctions in the following sentences.

1. The king died, and then the queen died.
2. She arrived at last, so we sat down to dinner.
3. It started raining harder, but we kept playing.
4. We can take the highway, or we can take the scenic route.
5. No one was listening, yet he kept talking.
6. I do not dislike sardines, nor do I dislike anchovies.

Correlative Conjunctions

Identify the correlative conjunctions in the following sentences.

1. Neither the king nor the queen died.
2. No sooner had he rubbed the lamp, than a genie appeared.
3. That bird is either a heron or a crane.
4. I don't know whether to play tennis or go bowling.
5. Not only did they paint the house, but also the garage.
6. I would rather go to the zoo than the circus.
7. Scarcely had I got in the tub when the phone rang.
8. Both the milk and the butter have passed their expiration dates.
9. George made a such a ridiculous remark that we all laughed.

10. That bottle of soda contains as much sugar as 110 eggs.

Subordinating Conjunctions

Identify the subordinating conjunctions in the following sentences.

1. Although Napoleon was only 5 feet 6 inches, tall, he was taller than the average Frenchman of his time.
2. The United States has no official language, even though people think it is English.
3. Humans landed on the moon before a patent was filed for a suitcase with wheels.
4. The Declaration of Independence has lasted so long in good condition because it was written on parchment, which is made from untanned animal skins.
5. When President Teddy Roosevelt was shot while giving a speech, he continued to the end of his speech, ninety minutes later.
6. Even if you have people in your dreams, you cannot invent faces for them.
7. Since people with creative minds find it harder to fall asleep, they prefer to stay up later
8. Was Benjamin Franklin not trusted to write the Declaration of Independence in order to prevent him from concealing a joke in it?
9. The stickers on fruit are made of edible paper so that if you eat one, you'll be fine.
10. Whenever January 1 in a leap year falls on a Sunday, January, April, and July will each have a Friday the 13th.

CHAPTER 7
CONJUNCTIONS: ANSWERS

Coordinating Conjunctions

1. and
2. so
3. but
4. or
5. yet
6. nor

Correlative Conjunctions

1. neither, nor
2. no sooner, than
3. either, or
4. whether, or
5. not only, but also
6. rather, than
7. scarcely, when
8. both, and
9. such, that
10. as, as

Subordinating Conjunctions

1. although
2. even though
3. before
4. because
5. when
6. even if
7. since
8. in order to
9 so that
10. whenever

INTERJECTIONS

WHAT IS AN INTERJECTION?

Oh my! Dear me! Help! Wow! Ugh! Ouch! Oops! Wow! Zap! Hey! Stop! These words are all interjections, the part of speech used to express emotion, give a warning, or catch someone's attention.

The word *interjection* comes from two Latin words: *inter* meaning "between " and *jacere, meaning "to throw." Interjection* is well named because an interjection is a word that is "thrown between" sentences or words in a sentence for the sole purpose of expressing an emotion. An interjection has no purpose in grammar It has no use in a sentence. In fact, sometimes it is set off by itself as a separate sentence (e.g., ”Help!" "Wow!”). Such sentences are called *exclamatory sentences.* They end in an exclamation point.

Position in Sentence

There is no rule about where to place an interjection in a sentence. Often it is placed at the beginning of a sentence, followed by a comma or exclamation point that separates it from the rest of the sentence.

Here are some more examples of interjections:

What!
Whoa!
Awesome!
Oh, no!
Bravo!

Hooray!
Alas!
Great!
Ah!
Awesome!
Woo-hoo!

Punctuation with Interjections

An interjection that expresses strong emotion is followed by an exclamation point. An interjection that expresses mild emotion is followed by a comma.

Examples:

1. Oh, I don't think so.
2. Oh! There's a snake!

Why isn't an exclamation point is used after *oh* in the first sentence? Because an exclamation point is used only if it indicates an emotional exclamation. In the first sentence, *oh* is simply an introductory word in a statement. The comma indicates that it is said without any particular emotion.

In the second sentence *oh* obviously is an exclamation of fright. Thus, it is followed by an exclamation point. The sentence, "There's a snake!" is likewise an exclamation and is followed by an exclamation mark to indicate this.

CHAPTER **8**

INTERJECTIONS: CHECK-UP

(Scroll down for answers.)

Which of the following words are *not* commonly used as interjections?

1. oh
2. wow
3. ugh
4. soft
5. cough
6. well
7. must
8. down
9. alas
10. ah

Supply an appropriate interjection word to express each of the emotions listed below.
1. joy
2. sorrow
3. surprise
4. anger
5. mild disappointment
6. fury
7. fatigue
8. suffering from pain
9. jubilation
10. despair

CHAPTER 8. INTERJECTIONS: ANSWERS

The following words are *not commonly* used as interjections: *soft, cough, must, down.*

Appropriate interjections for the emotions listed will vary. Check with a dictionary if you have a question about an emotion's meaning.

Jonathan Culver

INDEX

Author's Note

Dear Reader,

   Thank you for choosing *Easy English: The Parts of Speech.* If you enjoyed this book and found it useful, I'd like to ask a favor. Please leave a short review on the site where you bought the book. Reviews are incredibly useful in helping others find the kind of books they are looking for, and they take just a moment to leave.
   Authors really appreciate reviews, and I would love to get your feedback.
   Thank you so much!

Nancy Ragno

Join my monthly newsletter,
About English,
and get your
FREE proofreading guide.

Only available here.
Intriguing facts about English; tips on English usage; quizzes, quotes, exercises, jokes — and more. You can unsubscribe at any time.

This is the code to download your FREE guide:

https://BookHip.com/BAGVSRA

ABOUT THE AUTHOR

Nancy Ragno is an author of both adult and children's nonfiction books and co-author of *The World of Language,* a basal language arts textbook series for grades K-8 (previous editions: *Silver Burdett English* and *Silver Burdett & Ginn English*). She has been a teacher of grades 5 & 6, high school English, and adult education and was a senior editor and project editor at major publishing houses in New York, Boston, and Philadelphia.

Ragno lives in Baneberry, "the smallest city in Tennessee," (pop. 568), set on beautiful Douglas Lake at the foot of the Great Smoky Mountains. She is a member of the Tennessee Association for Family and Community Education and is a volunteer at Zoo Knoxville.

ZZZZZZZZZZ

NOTES